Because Sometimes Bureaucracy Gets in the Way

A collection of thoughts from the frontlines of Shadow IT

By Jeff Cave

Table of Contents

Introduction

Many years ago, I was working for an organization transitioning from being a small start-up with a new product to having been acquired by a large multinational corporation that wanted to push the product everywhere. As we started to expand, I found myself interacting with many newly graduated new hires. Minds with passion, intellect and energy, but sometimes struggled with what they perceived as resistance to change or pressures they had not been exposed to as students.

I found myself compelled to share the wisdom I had gained from my experiences with these young professionals. I believed that my insights could help them navigate the challenges they were facing and enhance their understanding of the field.

These individuals had many great ideas, but they often lacked the practical perspective of inter-office politics, customer expectations, and value-driven deliverables. They had studied fascinating concepts in school and were eager to implement them. This inspired me to find ways to share a more practical perspective, one that could help them turn their ideas into tangible solutions.

This book is a compilation of my observations and experiences in Information Systems over the years. It includes examples of non-optimal solutions that have propelled us forward in our quest for better solutions and insights into the intricate systems that shape our work environment and influence our goal of creating efficient systems.

Sometimes, they are just fun.

I wrote all of this hoping that people are just entering the industry because they are recent grads or managers trying to better understand the people around them.

It is probably worth noting that this is written by me, not a computer. In the world of LLM and generated content, I tried to keep my best human storytelling voice. I did reach out for help to AI, but I found it bland and sterile, so keep in mind: chapter title pages are AI; stories are all me.

At the end of the day, remember that computers were built to serve us, not the other way around.

Shit Disturbers
Reinvent the Wheel

- Redesigning solutions to fit problems is necessary

- Identifying the existence of problems is not a failure

- Bringing solutions to problems is the point of The Art

Automated testing of systems is my pet peeve: I think every computer system should have a series of tests that get run by another computer that tests every problem ever thought of. My current customer has asked me to start developing a system just like this for their record-keeping and delivery system.

Currently, the customer has purchased a third-party tool for automating control of the software, unfortunately, the tool sucks. It is very difficult for non-programmers to understand its roundabout logic (it uses screen-scraper-triggered events), and has no mechanism for managing large numbers of scripts (each one is managed in and of itself). When building testing systems,  the tests themselves tend to be easy to create; managing and tracking large numbers of tests becomes the problem.

Being a diligent consultant (alright, a diligent problem solver), I suggested it was possible to build a custom tool that wrapped the objects and was better able to be understood by non-programmers, allowing programmers to more easily manage a large number of tests.

Reinventing the Wheel

That's when I heard it:

> There's no point reinventing the wheel.

I take exception to this, I am encouraged to solve problems in the office and invention is the key to doing this. I recognize that all problems have been solved; we already have wheels. The only problem that ever exists is the need to refine the general solution to the particular instance of the problem; we need wheels suited to the current task.

If we had never reinvented the wheel we would still be driving around on Wagon Wheels. And ...

I myself like having soft rubber tires on my car.

In the end, we reinvent the wheel regularly, not every wheel is perfect for every vehicle. Similarly, when solving problems at the workplace designing systems, it is sometimes necessary to build a custom component that suits the needs of the problem.

While not a total reinvention, they are a design better suited to the problem at hand. To work around the foibles of the existing technology, just because the technology already exists, is the kind of short-sightedness that leads to <u>planes falling out of the sky</u>.

Shit Disturber

Naturally, the moment I suggest all of this, I am accused of being a Shit Disturber. But ...

> **When someone accuses me of being a Shit Disturber, I know I'm on the right track.**

Shit Disturber. Let's break that term down; "shit" and "disturber"; or a *disturber of shit*. For this to be true, there must be **shit** to be disturbed.

That I am being accused of being a *Shit Disturber* forces my audience to acknowledge that there is (in fact) *shit* present.

If there is *shit* present that has been ignored and avoided; it may be more important to ask questions like, When does somebody intend to do something about this *shit*? (This is usually the hardest part of convincing people to change: getting them to acknowledge that there is a problem which requires fixing.)

Being a **Disturber of Shit** is not a bad thing.

Just because you are disturbing the *shit*, does not mean you put it there.

If the *shit* is in the middle of the road, we can either ignore the *shit* or do something about it.

Naturally, this causes some discomfort: people have got used to their path around the *shit*; while it is being moved, the *shit* tends to stink; people have a hard enough time cleaning their own *shit* (let alone someone else's); and the person that put the *shit* there probably feels like *shit* for not cleaning it up in the first place.

The Disturber is just the person willing to do something about the problem. The fact of the matter is, that we can ignore problems for a long time, or put up with the temporary discomfort of fixing them.

Conclusion

Shit stinks and The Wheel turns; these are two truths of the world. Ignoring them does not make them go away.

In life, we need to identify problems (shit), find solutions (reinvent the wheel), and make the changes to enact those solutions (disturb the shit).

In the past, I have been both punished and praised for taking drastic action to solve drastic problems (often regarding the same problem and by the same person). While we may find change uncomfortable, we should never turn away from thesesolutions.

So a tip of the hat to all those Shit Disturbers out there; may you always keep finding ways to reinvent the wheel.

The John Deer Low-Down, wheel-driven, Manure Spreader
[Wikimedia, Public Domain]

16

Fun with Markov Network Brains

An introduction to evolutionary machine learning

Evolutionary machine learning algorithms are an expression of Darwinian Evolution

- A simple in-browser demonstration of an algorithm (Markov-Network Brains) is demonstrated

- Creating for creation's sake: creating solutions and simulations is an act of beauty

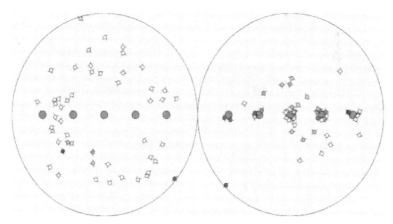

Over the course of about 1000 generations, a Markov Network Brain evolves dumb bugs (left) into something capable of finding food immediately (right). The bugs achieve this with no awareness of their environment beyond their physical bodies and antennae.

I was at my daughter's wedding, and (naturally) the conversation turned toward the capabilities and limitations of Artificial Intelligence.

I am not an AI expert, and my exposure to it has been sketchy at best. I have implemented algorithms but have never really done a deep dive into any of them to understand the mechanics. So, when the conversation brought up the concept of genetic or evolutionary algorithms, we both had to confess we didn't know that much about them.

What little we did discuss got me curious, and on the plane ride home, I came across an article on Markov Network Brains (MNB)[1]. When I first read about MNBs, something very deep resonated with past agriculture and medical experience, and I wanted to go deeper into the mechanics behind them.

A gut feeling of familiarity was only enough to whet my appetite; what I needed was a simple implementation that I could step through to observe the changes as they happened. I am a fan of Browser-side JavaScript for solving problems (there is always a compiler and debugger handy), so I was fortunate to stumble across an incomplete JavaScript implementation on GitHub.[2]

---

[1] The Adami Lab: Markov Network Brains
http://adamilab.msu.edu/markov-network-brains/
[2] Phillip Neal: MNB JS. As of publication, Neal has improved on his work and his take on the problem results in a different implemention style. Definitely worth comparing.
https://github.com/pnealgit/mnb_js

My initial intention was simply to step through the code to understand the process; however, after addressing a few minor visual bugs, I found I had over-tinkered, leaving me with some heavy lifting to get it to work. A deep tear-down was necessary and resulted in a fun little simulation.[3]

What better way to really understand what was going on?

A Layman's Description

Markov Network Brains are evolutionary algorithms based on the modern models of genetics and evolution. The same natural processes that allow bacteria to become drug-resistant can be used to breed animals for a specific purpose or *to breed a computer program well suited to solving a specific problem.*

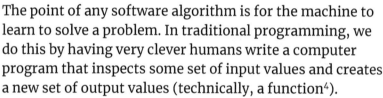

The point of any software algorithm is for the machine to learn to solve a problem. In traditional programming, we do this by having very clever humans write a computer program that inspects some set of input values and creates a new set of output values (technically, a function[4]).

MNBs (really Machine Learning algorithms in general) are no different: we have a problem that needs solving, a process for solving it, and we base it on some inputs. What differentiates an MNB is that we do not directly create the program; we allow it to be randomly generated, and slowly bring it closer to solving the problem by automatically

---

[3] https://jefferey-cave.gitlab.io/mnb-js-demo/
[4] Khan Academy: What is a function?
https://www.khanacademy.org/math/algebra/x2f8bb1159
5b61c86:functions/x2f8bb11595b61c86:evaluating-functi
ons/v/what-is-a-function

testing small random changes. (Actually, when phrased that way, it doesn't sound different at all[5])

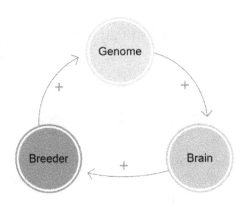

Three interrelated but independent components are essential to understanding MNBs: Genome, Brain, and Breeder. The ability of the algorithm to learn (become better able to solve the problem) is tied to the way three components work together:

1.   **Genome**: this is like the programmer's un-compiled code.

2.   **Brain**: one could think of this as an executable, compiled software. It also has memory allocated for storing information.

3.   **Breeder**: the developer, judging whether the code is successful or not

Like any software, these three parts are distinct but strongly interrelated. Also, like any software, the exciting parts happen at the transitions.

---

[5] Extreme Programming: Iterations (1999). Defines an iterative feedback approach to software project managment.
http://www.extremeprogramming.org/map/iteration.html

Genome Creation

The Genome is initially created as a random array [genome.js:23]. Like a DNA genome, this list will be used to build and recreate actors. In our case, it will be compiled into The Brain.

Genome → Brain

A Genome is compiled into a Brain by reading the Genome and using the data as the basis for allocating a quantity of memory, initializing the memory values, and allocating transforms for the memory [brain.js:18].

The transforms, or `gates`, are predefined functions like `or`, and, or `xor` transforms (other transforms are possible,[6] use your imagination) [gates.js:5]. Lastly, the Genome creates transforms that map the memory elements as inputs and outputs [brain.js:104].

Remember that these values were randomly generated, so (at least on the first pass) these transforms, and the quantity of memory are selected randomly. Basically, you have generated a completely random program acting on random memory elements.

An infinite number of monkeys typing on an infinite number of typewriters...

Brain → Breeding

---

[6] While simple logic gates have been implemented, Hintzelab describes several different types of transforms that can be used and are useful.
https://github.com/Hintzelab/MABE/wiki/Brain-Markov

Once The Brain has executed, it will have generated some outputs. It is up to The Breeder to judge whether the outputs were of any value or not, or more importantly, which of these executions were most valuable. In a more complex environment, it is reasonable for The Breeder to observe The Brain in action.

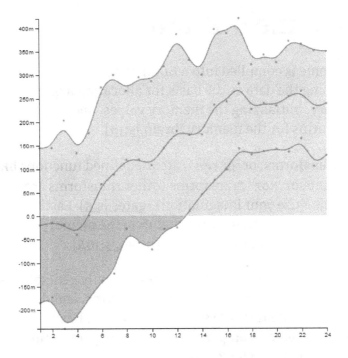

The score distribution of the bugs starts at -0.02σ0.2 and improves to 0.25σ0.1 after 24 generations. A plateau was reached at about generation 17.

To achieve this, we need to run several different Brains many times. Most of these runs will be useless, but some will be useful. Like an animal breeder, we can select the most valuable genomes and use them as the basis for better genomes, discarding the rest [evolve.js:55].

Breeding → Genome

Once The Breeder has selected the most successful programs, these programs can be used as the basis for trying new variations.

This is done through a reproduction process where genomes are randomly intermixed with one another (sexual reproduction) to produce a new algorithm that has a new mix of decision-making processes [evolve.js:93].

The key is that each of these newly created genomes is a little less random than its predecessors; suitable decision-making structures are *kept*, and bad ones are *culled*. Genomes identified as good are recombined with one another to see if they result in something even better. Over time, this process will result in progressively improving programs that get closer to solving the problem.

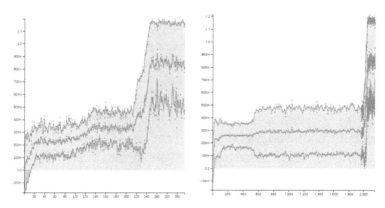

A second plateau was reached around generation 120, before the last improvement at around generation 230 (left) where it reached a score of 0.85σ0.2. Due to luck, a different run (right) took nearly 10 times longer to discover the second plateau.

Suggestions

As with any system that has randomness involved, debugging can be painful. Whether an observed behaviour results from luck (good or bad) or faulty programming.

The problem is most observable with bugs being randomly placed on top of food and then doing nothing. These bugs receive high rewards purely based on luck. Bugs actively moving in search of food end up being culled for not being as successful. This element of luck is undesirable.

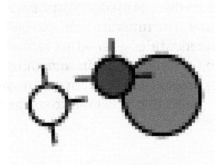

A lucky bug: the blue bug has no neural activity but was randomly populated right on top of a food source

As a result of pondering this problematic element of luck, two unique additions were added that are worth noting: the culling of useless brains and the reuse of successful genetics. Both of these are based on animal husbandry practices.

Early Culling

If the randomly generated program does not result in any output, it is useless to us.

The brains created are constrained to an array of approximately 50 elements of memory. Given 3 outputs, there is only a 6% chance that randomly generated programs will result in meaningful output. Larger memory will make these odds even worse.

To overcome this, I created a check in the generation routine. Immediately after creating a new brain, its transforms are scanned to determine if it will take any action [evolve.js:161]. If none of the transforms in the brain ever write to the output segment, the bug is immediately discarded, and a new bug is generated in its place [evolve.js:87].

Karma

While investigating the element of luck, it occurred to me that animal breeders keep track of their most successful breeding stock: animals with good parentage are likely to produce better offspring than animals with poor parentage. To simulate this, I introduced the concept of *karma*. Karma is a score attached to the genome rather than the bug itself. It is calculated at the end of a cycle by taking the bug's score and averaging it with its genome's score [evolve.js:32]. Newly created genomes inherit their predecessor's karmic score by averaging the score of parent genomes [evolve.js:101].

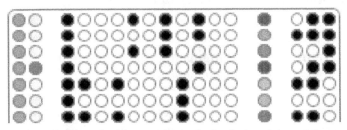

Each brain is monitored for activity to help distinguish activity and decision-making from luck. From left to right, the karma and bug score, sensors, memory state, and outputs (speed change, lean left, lean right)

When it comes time to compare the genomes for effectiveness, karma is used. Evaluating the overall genome rather than the bug itself allows unlucky genomes to get another chance to prove themselves. Continued lack of success will result in karma slowly declining (eventually resulting in a cull), while a single lousy generation will not cause an otherwise successful genome to be lost.

Unfortunately, I have no clear evidence that either of these were useful or effective, as these were introduced to compensate for what turned out to be a defect in the brain processing itself. While logically sound, it was developed due to a long delay in the first generation creation, believed to be caused by thousands of bugs being rejected. In hindsight, it was determined that this was not the actual cause, so there is no way to know if it made any difference.

Conclusion

At some point in my reading, I came across a statement that evolutionary programming has low value because similar results can be achieved faster using other techniques (there is a counter-argument that they can discover solutions humans cannot consider[7]). This may be true, but I had a lot of fun building this simulation and am still fascinated by Markov Network Brains.

Writing software is enjoyable. There is beauty and elegance to the processes involved that sometimes get lost in work deadlines and customer expectations. Occasionally, the act of writing software is just an expression of beauty and creativity. Playing with this simulation was just that, a bit of art for art's sake.

From a philosophical standpoint, genuinely understanding the evolutionary processes involved in this algorithm has given me a new perspective on complex, self-forming systems. From interpersonal relationships in the office to black-market economics, to the way students learn, to political alliances, I now see it slightly differently than I did.

It was interesting to watch my own biases in decision-making. My original hypothesis was that the bugs would evolve a spiral search pattern, and what I perceived as defects in their behaviour led me to increase punishment for touching the boundary to force them to conform. In the end, I was surprised to wake up one morning and discover the bugs had evolved a pattern of ignoring the pain and using the wall to orient themselves in their environment. My own little Stanford Experiment.

Lastly, this project has been a reminder of how useful it is to build throw-away programs. When learning something new, creating a small piece of code is better than tackling a giant problem. A small, simplified model can be held in your head while you learn. When your organization requires a *reliable* solution, reach for a battle-tested library; build from scratch, when you want to *understand*.

---

[7] https://en.wikipedia.org/wiki/Evolved_antenna

To quote Feynman:

What I cannot create, I do not understand

-- Feynman[8]

Deep understanding is a funny thing; sometimes, you come to learn that the battle-tested library isn't as helpful as you thought.

Your Next Steps

If you are interested in Markov Network Brains, you should

1. Open the simulation[9]

2. Press F12

3. Put a break-point somewhere in the code

4. Start stepping through it

Stepping through running code and observing the changes is the best way to learn about a program's behaviour.

---

[8] Ironically? Poetically? I found that quote via Chris Adami's blog while searching for the references for this article ... Adami is the guy who started this whole mess for me
https://adamilab.blogspot.com/2013/02/your-conscious-you.html
[9] https://jefferey-cave.gitlab.io/mnb-js-demo/

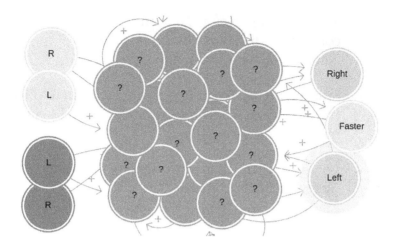

Fork and Fix

A co-worker was asking me about this program and started suggesting all kinds of great ideas I could implement to make it more interesting.I suddenly realized I had taken everything I wanted from this little toy. I'm going to move on to other projects. Instead, I suggested **he should make the changes**!

Fork the project from the same point I did[10], and build it yourself. Or Fork my version[11] and make a cool modification ... either way, I would love to see what you come up with.

- Change the physics (collisions, spherical world, ...)

---

[10] The exact point that was forked from has a more direct approach
https://gitlab.com/jefferey-cave/mnb-js-demo/tree/newer_think/www/js
[11] Modifications I made include a more object oriented aproach
https://gitlab.com/jefferey-cave/mnb-js-demo/tree/master/www/js

- Make the bugs aware of one another (watch competitive behaviour evolve? cooperative behaviour?)

- Find a more challenging problem for them to solve (randomize the food, introduce fight and flight to make them prey, ...)

- Put the brain in a separate thread[12] (someone please do this) or on the GPU[13].

- Probabilistic Logic vs Binary

- ... trust me: the list could go on forever ...

Further Reading

You could also read more about Markov Network Brains from people who actually know what they are talking about. I have taken some liberties with the metaphors I have used, and learning the shared metaphors and terminology would also be helpful.

- Adami Labs[14]: The original article that I found. Also has a battle-tested C++ library available

---

[12] Mozilla Developer Documenation, WebWorkers
https://developer.mozilla.org/en-US/docs/Web/API/Web_Workers_API/Using_web_workers
[13] WebGL Fundamentals, offers a series of tutorials on how to use GPUs from the browser
https://webglfundamentals.org/
[14] The Adami Lab, Markov Network Brains
https://adamilab.msu.edu/markov-network-brains/

- Brain.js[15]: A battle-tested JS library that implements MNBs as one of its models

- Wikipedia: Markov Logic Network[16]

- Modular Agent Based Evolution Framework[17]: MABE (python) offers an interesting framework for defining all the parts (battle-tested)

- Reddit[18]: A Detailed Criticism of Evolutionary Algorithms/Computation by Programmers?

---

[15] Brain.js: GPU accelerated Neural networks in JavaScript, for Browsers and Node.js
https://brain.js.org/

[16] https://en.wikipedia.org/wiki/Markov_logic_network

[17]
https://github.com/Hintzelab/MABE/wiki/MABE-framework

[18]
https://www.reddit.com/r/compsci/comments/4hwui7/deleted_by_user/

Build a Chromolabe

Understanding algorithms and automated decision making, using some coloured pencils and paper

- Computational algorithms represent automated decision-making tools

- Distinct colour selection is a common problem in data visualization

- A mechanical device is demonstrated to show how a machine can make decisions

- Suitable for ages 12 to 120

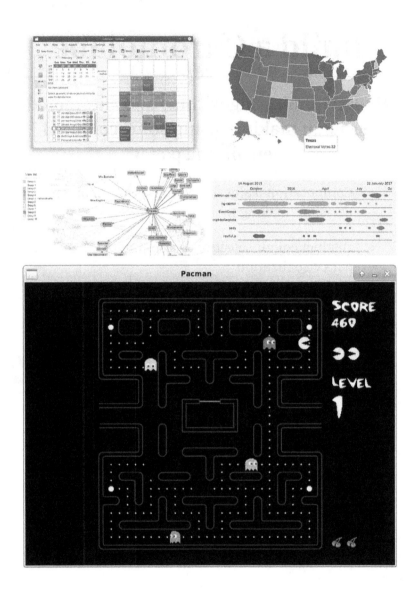

Classes from my personal calendar, D3 map choropleth, force directed graph, gantt style chart, or an open source knock off of a popular video game.

Most people rely on their natural human intuition for decision-making, and human intuition is based on interacting with the physical world around us. Computers, on the other hand, deal in abstract ideas, something humans just aren't well equipped to deal with.

What goes on inside a computer's mind is a mystery to most people. It is scary: you can't see, touch, or taste it. This makes it hard to understand what programmers are doing and, therefore, can be intimidating for people.

This means that programming is constrained to the realm of people with "a freakish knack for manipulating abstract symbols".[19] This activity is designed to help bridge that gap. We are going to build a physical computer.

Computer programmers are often faced with the daunting task of taking those abstract concepts and making them concrete for their audience, a tricky and detailed task.

One of the tools used to do this is colour.

Colour is often used to visualise the categorisation of ideas: time blocks in a calendar, political parties, characters in a game, we use colour everywhere to group related things together.

As programmers, we have just encountered our first problem: how do we choose the colour palette we will use in our program?

---

[19] Kill Math, Bret Victor, 2011-04-11
https://worrydream.com/KillMath

Good Palettes

There are three components to selecting a good colour palette for use in visualizations:

1. High Differentiation
2. Sufficient Colours
3. Aesthetically Pleasing

Every colour palette used in a visualization should maintain these three essential elements.

Sufficient Colours

There should be enough colours to meet the needs of the visualisation.

In the early days of video games, it was often enough to have 4 different colours: one for each player. In cartography, the number of colours needed is dictated by the number of shared borders; the same colour should never touch.

Sufficient is different depending on what you are trying to represent.

High Differentiation

The colours used should be sufficiently different so people can tell them apart. If a driver tries to tell the difference between "stop" and "go" at a traffic intersection, there should be **no** ambiguity in which colour is being seen by the audience.

Finding food in the wilderness is a matter of survival for hunter/gatherer humans. The differentiation of colour is built-in in humans. [image: Wikimedia]

This problem is complicated by internationalization (colour means different things in different cultures), biological issues (colour blindness), and many other issues (this isn't a simple process).

Aesthetically Pleasing

At the end of the day, humans are the ones who will be looking at this visualization; they should find it pleasing to look at.

Choosing complementary colours can often have bizarre visual consequences. We need to work with the way humans are built. There is also a fashionable element to this, colours that are popular today may not be popular tomorrow.

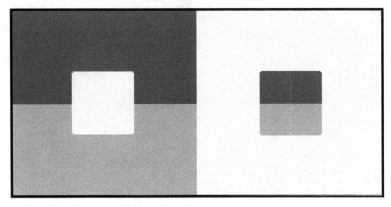

Complimentary colours have high contrast but, when placed side-by-side, can have negative consequences. Interestingly, the pastel variants do not suffer these consequences.

Infinite Colours to Choose

Choosing colours is difficult.

There are an infinite number of colours to choose from, but we need to select just 4-12 colours, which need to meet our three requirements.

Complex decision-making is exactly what we build machines to help us with. To start building our information machine, we need to first organize everything we know; all we know so far is a fundamental truth of the universe:

There are a lot of colours to choose from

To help us sort through the options, we need some way of organizing them. That is a fundamental thing programmers do; they organize stuff. By organizing things, we can simplify our problems.

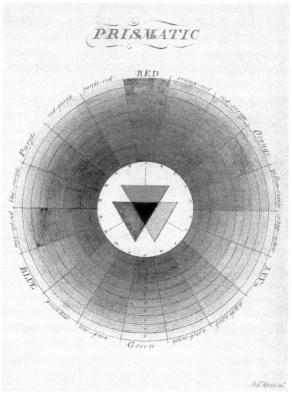

Moses Harris, The Natural System of Colours (1776) [Wikipedia: Color Wheel] Colour wheels have long been a tool for grouping similar colours.

So we first need to narrow the set down; let's only pick from colours humans can see: this process can be represented with a Colour Wheel.

Colour wheels represent the variations of colours that can be made by mixing different base colours together. The base colours are placed around the outside.

While not representative of every colour possible, these colour wheels give us many colours. They also have the advantage of placing similar colours physically close together.

This helps us satisfy two of our requirements:

1. **Sufficient**: If we need many, there are many.

2. **Differentiation**: the further they are physically, the more different they are.

Mechanically Making Decisions

Narrowing down an infinite number of colours to just the 4-6 we need is complex, and building a machine to choose for us is the point of the exercise. Unfortunately, describing the machine and how it works mathematically sounds like a bunch of abstract symbol manipulation.

Rather than trying to explain it, let the demonstration be its own proof. Besides, this machine is really simple...

... like ... *really* simple.

Building the machine is way easier than explaining it. Once you make it, how the colour picker works should become evident.

1. Gather your supplies

Get a pencil... sharper is better. Also, make a colour wheel, and trace out a blank circle on a separate sheet of paper.

2. Draw a Spiral

Using the blank circle, starting anywhere along the outside, begin tracing it gently with your pencil. When you have a *feel* for the circle, draw an evenly-spaced spiral toward the middle.

3. Do the calculation

Place your pencil on the topmost tick-mark of the circle.

Now, move your pencil three steps, and mark the position:

1. across the circle, to the opposite side

2. over one tick-mark (either way)

1. move in one step toward the middle

2. mark that position

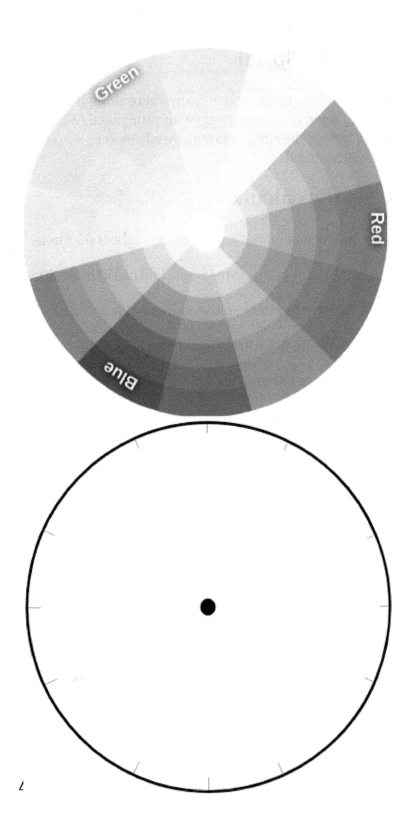

Now, starting from this new position,

1. move across to the opposite side

2. move over one tick-mark (same direction)

3. move in two steps toward the middle

4. mark that position

Did you see it? The slight change in the repeating pattern?

Keep moving around, marking points on the chart until you reach the middle.

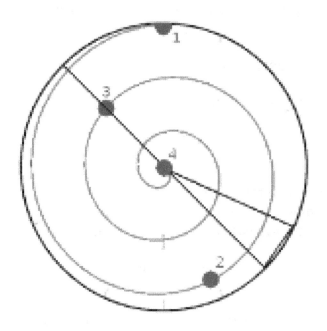

One of the reasons we like machines is they do repetitive tasks for us. Describing the repetitive tasks is often the real trick

4. Make it permanent

When you think you have all your dots in the correct location, carefully...

(make sure you are careful; this is both delicate and dangerous)

place your pencil over the first dot and...

(don't mess it up: we are building computers here)

Ram that pencil through!

Seriously, don't be gentle. Punch a good-sized hole in the paper.

(just be careful not to put your hand in the way)

Do that for each of the dots you made.

Reading the Results

Align your spiral graph with the colour wheel, and watch your colour palette reveal itself. Start from the first dot and copy down each colour your program chose.

That is your unique colour palette to use in your visualizations.

Remember when we started, we were looking for a colour palette that satisfied three criteria:

1. High Differentiation

2. Sufficient Colours

3. Aesthetically Pleasing

High Differentiation

By starting with a colour wheel, we locate similar colours physically close together. Our algorithm then travels far across to select physically far apart colours.

Sufficient Colours

The spiral pattern ensures that we never select the same colour twice. No matter how many colours we choose, we always have different colours.

You may notice that the differentiation of colours decreases as you approach the middle: the more colours you pick, the more similar they get. This is a compromise we need to make. It is a balance between having a lot and having them be different.

Aesthetically Pleasing

This is always tough; what is pleasing to me may not be pleasing to you.

There is no way to have our simple computer decide whether the selected colour is pretty or not. That is something best left to humans. So take a good look at your colours, and determine if you like them. You may have gotten a good starting point by luck, but maybe you did not.

One last thing you should try: poke a small hole right in the middle.

Now, you can rotate the selector wheel around the colour wheel to fine-tune your selection process.

Conclusion

Don't just read about it, do it.

This is a simple activity that lets a person feel how programming works. Have a younger sibling? Do it with them, and watch how they see the activity come to life because that is part of programming, too: helping people see the value of automated decision-making.

Variations

I recommend physically making your own colour wheel with pencil crayons or watercolour. You could draw a colour wheel programmatically. All of it should be hand-drawn to maximize comprehension.

A natural extension of this is to write a function (*programmatic* or *algebraic*) to pick the colour. This would require you to define the colour wheel space and traverse the space in a spiral. HTML colour codes based on RGB make a good return value.

If you want a challenge, move into a more complete 3-dimensional colour space. RGB defines three dimensions: a function that selects from a *colour sphere*, with a 3-dimensional spiral search of the space... even I'm not sure how.

Further Reading

While this represents one way to select a colour palette, it is not necessarily the best. Have a look at some other considerations:

Color Wheel Pro: <u>Color Theory Basics</u>

 Graphiq: <u>Finding the Right Color Palettes for Data Visualizations</u>

 <u>A color palette optimized for data visualization</u>

When I came up with the idea for constructing this contraption, I was thinking about the

 <u>Astrolabe</u>: a computer from the first century, developed in Alexandria.

If you are looking for a digital variation of this tool

 Adobe: <u>Color Wheel</u>

Though I suspect building it yourself would be more fun.

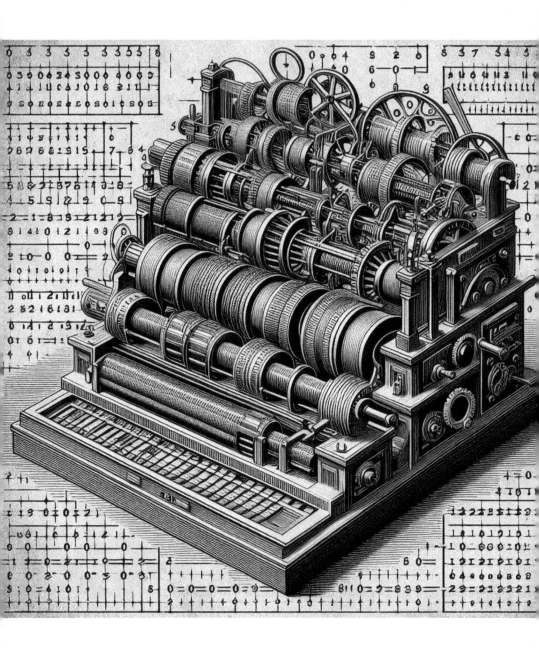

Using WebGL to Solve a Practical Problem

An introduction for Dummy Programmers (using the Smith-Waterman Algorithm)

- An explanation of why GPUs can significantly increase processing speed

- A simple demonstration of a GPU implementation

 Complete Code @ codesandbox

Some time ago, I was teaching introductory Python and basic browser programming. During this time, I wrote an 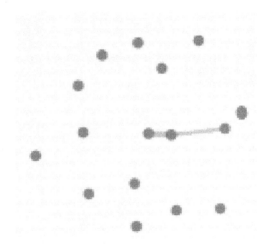application that compares pieces of software code and presents their similarity[20] in a force-directed and tornado diagram. I ran this software semi-regularly (weekly), and a significant problem appeared with my solution very early on.

It took a really long time to solve. A **really** long time. A **painfully** long time.

I needed to find a way to speed up the processing.

The points are student submissions, and the lines represent the level of similarity. With 36 comparisons, this takes … long enough that I get bored.

When I wrote the tool, GPU processing was hot, and everyone was talking about how this would speed up *everything*. No matter what the question, GPU was the

---

[20] https://jefferey-cave.gitlab.io/miss/

answer. This was an obvious avenue of investigation. However, I had decided to write this tool in the browser (legal and ethical constraints), and browsers do not have direct access to the underlying hardware.

So, if all the cool kids are using GPUs, and this is written in the browser, I'm intensely curious ... it looks like I'm learning WebGL and GLSL.[21]

Pre-Requisites

Before beginning, you should be comfortable with programming. The demonstration is written in vanilla Browser JavaScript, so no particularly advanced techniques are used; however, using WebGL requires switching between two languages and compiling code. Web programming does not usually involve those things.

The only programmatic technique you should be vaguely familiar with would be cellular automaton: Conway's Game of Life is the classic example of this. GoL has been a staple of programming instructors for 50 years because the problem is relatively simple, the solution is complex enough to exercise student skills, and the output is fun.

In addition, I strongly recommend going to the local office supply store and buying a cheap pencil, eraser, and pad of grid paper. Nothing builds understanding like working through problems yourself.

---

[21] MDN Web Docs, GLSL Shaders
https://developer.mozilla.org/en-US/docs/Games/Techni
ques/3D_on_the_web/GLSL_Shaders

How GPUs Speed Up Processing

GPUs are a completely distinct mechanism from CPUS. CPUs are designed in such a way as to offer many operations to people and allows you to run them one at a time. GPUs offer fewer operations, but set them up so you can run a bunch of them simultaneously (parallel processing).

This comes at a couple of different costs to us programmers.

1. It's like working on a different computer.

2. The instructions we write for one don't necessarily exist for the other.

That's annoying, but ... parallel processing: as long as they all run the same set of instructions, you can run a calculation a couple of thousand times, except simultaneously. Very simply put:

GPUs do parallel processing of a single function.

Technically, the function is called a "kernel"; I referred to it as a program in my code.

Consider the following function:

```
function MultiplicationTable(size=10){
   let table = Allocate2DArray(size);
   for(memLoc.x=0; memLoc.x < list.length; memLoc.x++){
     for(memLoc.y=0; memLoc.y < list.length; memLoc.y++){
       table[memLoc.x][memLoc.y] = memLoc.x * memLoc.y;
     }
   }
   return table;
}
```

Parallel processing on the GPU is about doing the same action simultaneously. In this case, the multiplication is a process that is consistently the same.

I will do some basic math: a 10 x 10 array costs us 100 units of processing time.

Now consider doing the same processing using the GPU

```
function MultiplicationTable(size=10){
   let table = Allocate2DArray(size);
   table = gpu(table)
     .forEach((memLoc)=>{return memLoc.x * memLoc.y;});
   return table;
}
```

That forEach costs one (1) unit of processing time, no matter whether it is 10x10 or 10000x10000.

I made that code up. It won't work, but it does give you some idea of what we are trying to work toward. No matter how big we make `table`, it will take 1 unit of processing time.

Using GPUs

GPUs are mechanically different from CPUs.

Because of this mechanical difference, it is helpful to think of GPUs as a completely separate computer you are attached to. Not only do you have an individual processing unit (GPU instead of CPU), but it also uses separate memory and a separate instruction set.

These three elements of separation mean there are three primary phases that we need to go through to make use of them:

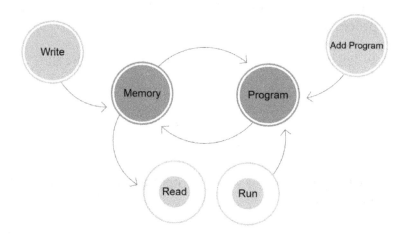

1. Send the instructions in the GPU space (compilation)

2. Exchange memory with the GPU space (transfer — read/write)

3. Execute the instructions (execution)

Managing these three phases is WebGL's most challenging and complex part. There are a significant number of details that need to be handled just to exchange information with the other space.

Part of this is because the 'G' in GPU and WebGL stands for Graphics. We are using something designed for manipulating images to do general computation. The details that need to be managed revolve around defining elements of an image; this means we need to describe our raw numbers in terms of an image.

This is simplified by creating helper functions that describe our data.

psGPU

A helper class was set up in the demonstration called psGPU [webgl.html:158]. It has a few functions that abstract much of the configuration away:

addProgram

Compiles and sends a block of GLSL code (as a string) to the GPU space. [webgl.html:384-456]

initMemory

Creates a hidden "image" that will act as our processing memory [webgl.html:289-346]

write

Transfers our memory (UInt8Array) over to the GPU space [webgl.html:254-263]

`read`

Transfers our memory back from the GPU space
[webgl.html:241-252]

`run`

executes the program we compiled [webgl.html:266-287]

As a novice, these functions became critical to setting up the GPU. I was intensely interested in implementing an algorithm, and the complexities of memory management significantly distracted the complexity I wanted to focus on.

pixel

At some point, a second helper class was created called `pixel`. [webgl.html:96]

The interchanged memory through read and write consists of a byte array. Interpreting an image as a byte array calls for a few more helpers. In particular, each image pixel is interpreted as 4 bytes, representing the pixel's Red, Green, Blue, and Alpha (`rgba`)[22] values. Within the GPU, these values are defined by the type `vec4`, a collection of 4 values (r,g,b,a).

The pixel class was created to help maintain consistent naming across the CPU/GPU boundary. It is just a convenience for mapping the returned `UInt8Array` to the 4 bytes representing a given pixel, allowing them to be referred to by the same `rgba` notation.[webgl.html:102-110]

----

[22] MDN Web Docs, Color, RGBA
https://developer.mozilla.org/en-US/docs/Web/CSS/color
_value#rgba%28%29

DrawGrid

The most interesting (maybe "useful" is a better word) utility function is `DrawGrid`. [webgl.html:828-883]

Because GPUs are designed to manage images, the only inspection of memory changes available is by looking at a picture. Since the purpose of this project has nothing to do with images, colour is not a meaningful representation. This makes debugging ... trickier.

To help, `DrawGrid` only renders each pixel location as its underlying numeric value. It is roughly equivalent to JavaScript's `console.log`, allowing the developer to dump a set of values to a visible location for inspection.

It is most effectively used by placing it (and a break-point) immediately after a kernel `run`. Remember to comment it out when measuring speed.

Actually Running

Once the helpers are in place, defining our processing functions and calling them in the correct order is a simple matter.

1. Send the instructions in the GPU space

2. Exchange memory with the GPU space

3. Execute the instructions

Given the amount of helper code in place, few instructions are left to perform in the actual code portion on the CPU side. The really interesting logic *should* be moved to the GPU; all the interesting processing *should* reside in the kernel definitions.

On the CPU side, we send the instructions to the GPU (`addProgram`) and then repeatedly send notifications to execute the function (`run`).

The General Problem

Comparing code for similarity is a well-solved problem. Comparing sequences of instructions while considering minor variations sounds very similar to DNA comparisons.

In genetics, sequence alignment algorithms have been around for a long time (Needleman-Wunsch dating to about 1970). Comparing DNA sequences for similarity while considering minor variations due to mutation or cross-over is a common goal, which is the same problem we are trying to solve. Think of this as a paternity test for software.

In my case, I reached for a Smith-Waterman comparison.

The best way to understand an algorithm is to solve it with pencil and paper. In this case, I spent much time with a pencil, eraser, and pad of grid paper from the local convenience store.

Take the names of two animals: coelecanth and pellican.[23]

---

[23] Not the BioInformatics class I took, but a good slide on the subject. Contained the example of pelican and coelecanth. It is worth noting that the spelling of "Pelican" is incorrect in the demonstration. This is the present author's error, but does exemplify the pattern matching capabilities. https://slideplayer.com/slide/5142106/16/images/21/Smith-Waterman-Algorithm.jpg

On the surface, they do not appear similar; however, closer inspection (surprisingly) shows they do align reasonably well:

```
c o e . l e c a n t h
p . e l l i c a n
```

Programmatically, we can find this alignment by solving a Smith-Waterman matrix:

	P_0		E_1		L_2		L_3		I_4		C_5		A_6		N_7	
C_0	0	0	0	0	0	0	0	0	0	0	2	0	0	0	0	0
	3	0	3	0	3	0	3	0	3	0	3	1	2	0	3	0
O_1	0	0	0	0	0	0	0	0	0	0	0	0	0	0	0	0
	3	0	3	0	3	0	3	0	3	0	1	0	3	0	3	0
E_2	0	0	2	0	0	0	0	0	0	0	0	0	0	0	0	0
	3	0	3	1	2	0	3	0	3	0	3	0	3	0	3	0
L_3	0	0	0	0	2	0	2	0	0	0	0	0	0	0	0	0
	3	0	1	0	3	2	2	3	2	2	2	1	2	0	3	0
A_4	0	0	0	0	0	0	0	0	0	0	0	0	2	0	0	0
	3	0	3	0	1	1	1	2	3	2	3	1	3	2	2	1
C_5	0	0	0	0	0	0	0	0	0	0	2	0	0	0	0	0
	3	0	3	0	1	0	1	1	3	1	3	3	2	2	3	1
A_6	0	0	0	0	0	0	0	0	0	0	0	0	2	0	0	0
	3	0	3	0	3	0	1	0	3	0	1	2	3	4	2	3
N_7	0	0	0	0	0	0	0	0	0	0	0	0	0	0	2	0
	3	0	3	0	3	0	3	0	3	0	1	1	1	3	3	5
T_8	0	0	0	0	0	0	0	0	0	0	0	0	0	0	0	0
	3	0	3	0	3	0	3	0	3	0	1	0	1	2	1	4
H_9	0	0	0	0	0	0	0	0	0	0	0	0	0	0	0	0
	3	0	3	0	3	0	3	0	3	0	3	0	1	1	1	3

To understand how this alignment can be solved mechanically, I recommend following the <u>example given on Wikipedia</u>. I don't mean go read the Wikipedia page; I mean pull out that grid paper and reproduce the example for yourself. Solve each step and verify it against the example. If you made a mistake, spend some time understanding your error, and start over.

When you can solve a Smith-Waterman for yourself, you have proof that you understand it.

While the implementation is discussed in detail below, it is worth having an intuitive understanding of one of the two processes involved; trying to learn both simultaneously is harder. If you are interested in implementing algorithms on the GPU, already understanding the example algorithm is useful. If you are already a master of the GPU and are interested in implementing Smith-Watermans, this basic example may be a good stepping stone.

Put it together

It isn't easy. Using the GPU requires us to think in parallel, and this requires us to think in ways that we aren't usually used to. Things we take for granted in linear processing aren't available to us; things we would typically avoid, we accept for the sake of being able to use the tool.

The idea for how to do this actually came from one of my favourite college assignments: Conway's Game of Life (GoL). In GoL, each life-form location changes its state based on the state of its nearest neighbours. This is usually solved in a grid represented by a table of values on the screen.

The key to that statement is that each automata cell has a state resolved independently of all the others and based on the values of its nearest neighbours. That pretty much describes the Smith-Waterman as well. The only real change is that Smith-Watermans only consider the neighbouring cells in the upper-left corner (North, West, and North-West).

These parent values need to be calculated prior to being able to calculate values, representing one of the challenges of parallelizing the algorithm: you cannot calculate dependent values in parallel. The first mental breakthrough was an animated GIF I found online that demonstrated a diagonal parallelization of values in an SW matrix.(the original reference is lost to the recesses of memory now)

This was compounded by the fact that I had initially optimized my algorithm for low memory consumption. To do this, I maximized the early release of the memory associated with a given cell if it was not part of a chain. One of the challenges in using a GPU was determining how to arrange the memory so that calculations were only performed on elements with a complete parent set.

	P_0		E_1		L_2		L_3		I_4		C_5		A_6		N_7	
C_0	0	0	0	0	0	0	0	0	0	0	2	0	0	0	0	0
	3	0	3	0	3	0	3	0	3	0	3	1	2	0	3	0
O_1	0	0	0	0	0	0	0	0	0	0	0	0	0	0	0	0
	3	0	3	0	3	0	3	0	3	0	1	0	3	0	3	0
E_2	0	0	2	0	0	0	0	0	0	0	0	0	0	0	0	0
	3	0	3	1	2	0	3	0	3	0	3	0	3	0	3	0
L_3	0	0	0	0	2	0	2	0	0	0	0	0	0	0	0	0
	3	0	1	0	3	2	2	3	2	2	2	1	2	0	3	0
A_4	0	0	0	0	0	0	0	0	0	0	0	0	2	0	0	0
	3	0	3	0	1	1	1	2	3	2	3	1	3	2	2	1
C_5	0	0	0	0	0	0	0	0	0	0	2	0	0	0	0	0
	3	0	3	0	1	0	1	1	3	1	3	3	2	2	3	1
A_6	0	0	0	0	0	0	0	0	0	0	0	0	2	0	0	0
	3	0	3	0	3	0	1	0	3	0	1	2	3	4	2	3
N_7	0	0	0	0	0	0	0	0	0	0	0	0	0	0	2	0
	3	0	3	0	3	0	3	0	3	0	1	1	1	3	3	5
T_8	0	0	0	0	0	0	0	0	0	0	0	0	0	0	0	0
	3	0	3	0	3	0	3	0	3	0	1	1	1	3	1	5
H_9	0	0	0	0	0	0	0	0	0	0	0	0	0	0	0	0
	3	0	3	0	3	0	3	0	3	0	3	0	1	1	1	3

Working diagonally allows us to maintain sufficient parent cells (green) to calculate the number of child cells (yellow) in parallel. Processing this on the GPU means that all of the other cells (white) will be calculated for no reason. A reasonable trade-off.

This focus on optimization blinded me to the fact that the cost of evaluating a matrix with a GPU is 1, regardless of the matrix size. The original speed using CPU calculations required that every cell be evaluated one at a time: `width * height` processing time. Using the GPU and calculating all of the elements each time felt like wasteful work, but at some point, the realization it was still only `width +`

`height` processing time dawned on my dummy programmer brain.

Who cares about wasting a bunch of processing *effort* when it saves that much *time*!?

While I'm sure there are efficiencies to be gained, they are insignificant compared to the speed increases of just evaluating cells needlessly until the entire matrix is solved.

Once this situation is accepted, it becomes reasonable to create the GPU function (or kernel) smithwaterman that can solve for an individual 2-D matrix cell [webgl:528-586]. An initialization routine was also created, calculating the initial match value [webgl:687-710].

The first thing to note is the entire program is passed to addProgram as a `string`. This is to allow the GPU to compile the code, but unfortunately, it means no syntax highlighting. It also leads to very cryptic messages about invalid syntax. As you make changes, make them small to ensure you can identify where a syntax error was made.

The implementation of the algorithm itself is minimal.

Initialize the Memory

Before we can start acting on values, we need to transfer the values to the GPU. While addProgram is used to write the code to the GPU, writing memory is performed by the write function. We start by fetching an appropriately sized array and then filling only the array's top and left portions [webgl:735-744]. This minimizes CPU cycles by leaving the iterative portion to the GPU.

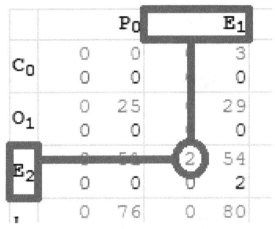

	P_0			E_1
C_0	0	0		3
	0	0		0
O_1	0	25		29
	0	0		0
E_2			②	54
	0	0		2
	0	76	0	80

The initial Matrix score is done by comparing the extreme North and West values. Matches get a base score of 2 while everything else is set to 0.

Our first GPU task (`initializeSpace`) is to compare the intersections of these values for matches [webgl:687-710]. For each cell, we look at the value to the extreme west and north [webgl:700] and assign 2 points for a match or 0 points for a mismatch [webgl:707]. This score is stored on the red channel.

It is worth noting that the GPU does its processing in terms of fractional values (`float`): everything is a portion of 1. So, while the scores are intended to be the integer values 0 and 2, these must be consumed as some proportion. The values are passed to the function as `0.0/255.0` and `2.0/255.0`, making them easily convertible between a `UInt8` and `float`.

This is an important thing to remember. For the purposes of this algorithm:

Everything on the GPU side treats the numbers as floats, but the returned memory is an integer.

Solve the Matrix

Smith-Watermans construct a chain of values representing the best matches. In this case, "best" is the neighbour with the highest running score.

The first step is to look up the nearest neighbours, which requires us to determine how close those neighbours are. The GPU thinks in fractional values (`float`), while we think in discrete values (`int`). We need to calculate the fractional size of a memory location (a `pixel`) [webgl:544]. Once this is done, we can look up the value of the current cell (`here`) and its nearest neighbours (`nw`, `n`, `w`) [webgl:548].

Once we have identified the critical neighbours, we can assess their values. This is done by checking all three for the highest score and temporarily storing it on the `blue` channel [webgl:562].

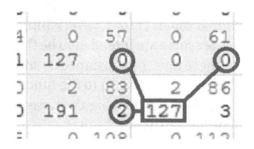

Looking at the nearest neighbours (yellow) we can determine the direction of the match. In this case horizontal (127) is the best match. Values are stored as fractions of 255 (255/2 → 127).

Knowing which score was highest allows us to determine which direction forms the chain; each direction is tested to see if it forms the desired chain. In the event of a tied score, diagonal matches should be favoured because horizontal and vertical matches represent a skip; horizontal and vertical ties can be resolved arbitrarily. Directionality is represented by enumerations of `1-north`, `2-west`, and `3-northwest` and is stored on the `blue` channel [webgl:568].

Knowing the direction of the chain, we can now tally up the running total. The running score of the chain is added to the local matching score; logically, this is done after the direction is recorded; however, due to only having 4 memory locations per cell, it is pulled from the temporary value stored on the blue channel before we finalize direction [webgl:565]. We also apply a skip penalty (-1 point) to chains that had to perform a skip operation (non-diagonal direction) [webgl:579].

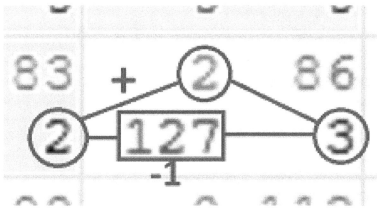

Having identified the parent, we can add the running score, to the local score, and apply any skip penalties. In this case (2+2-1), which then gets stored on the current alpha channel.

Once the calculation is complete, the values are stored permanently to the current cell in the `alpha` channel [webgl:584]. It is worth reviewing that there are 4 memory locations per cell and how we have allocated them:

- **red**: local matching score

- **green**: unused (reserved for future use)

- **blue**: chain direction

- **alpha**: chain score

Cycle: 8

	P_0	E_1	L_2	L_3	I_4	C_5	A_6	N_7
C_0	0 0 / 3 0	0 0 / 3 0	0 0 / 3 0	0 0 / 3 0	0 0 / 3 0	2 0 / 3 1	0 0 / 2 0	0 0 / 3 0
O_1	0 0 / 3 0	0 0 / 3 0	0 0 / 3 0	0 0 / 3 0	0 0 / 3 0	0 0 / 1 0	0 0 / 3 0	0 0 / 3 0
E_2	0 0 / 3 0	2 0 / 3 1	0 0 / 2 0	0 0 / 3 0	0 0 / 3 0	0 0 / 3 0	0 0 / 3 0	0 0 / 3 0
L_3	0 0 / 3 0	0 0 / 1 0	2 0 / 3 2	2 0 / 2 3	0 0 / 2 2	0 0 / 2 1	0 0 / 2 0	0 0 / 3 0
A_4	0 0 / 3 0	0 0 / 3 0	0 0 / 1 1	0 0 / 1 2	0 0 / 3 2	0 0 / 3 1	2 0 / 3 2	0 0 / 2 1
C_5	0 0 / 3 0	0 0 / 3 0	0 0 / 1 0	0 0 / 1 1	0 0 / 3 1	2 0 / 3 3	0 0 / 2 2	0 0 / 3 1
A_6	0 0 / 3 0	0 0 / 3 0	0 0 / 3 0	0 0 / 1 0	0 0 / 3 0	0 0 / 1 2	2 0 / 3 4	0 0 / 2 3
N_7	0 0 / 3 0	0 0 / 3 0	0 0 / 3 0	0 0 / 3 0	0 0 / 3 0	0 0 / 1 1	0 0 / 1 3	0 0 / 3 5
T_8	0 0 / 3 0	0 0 / 3 0	0 0 / 3 0	0 0 / 3 0	0 0 / 3 0	0 0 / 1 1	0 0 / 1 3	0 0 / 1 5
H_9	0 0 / 3 0	0 0 / 3 0	0 0 / 3 0	0 0 / 3 0	0 0 / 3 0	0 0 / 3 0	0 0 / 1 1	0 0 / 1 3

This diagram shows the calculation wave as it moves across the matrix. Green values represent cells with sufficient information to solve, yellow values represent values that have settled into their final state, and white values are ones that are indeterminate. Every cell is calculated on every cycle. Using this pattern, we can reduce the number of required cycles from `x*y` to `x+y`.

As noted earlier, it is not sufficient to execute this process once. While we are calculating every cell's chain score, there is insufficient information for the last cell to complete its chain calculation until it's neighbours have completed their calculation. To resolve this, we run the GPU processing multiple times, first calculating the worst-case number of cycles required [webgl:518] and then sending processing signals to the GPU in a loop [webgl:752]. Each iteration of GPU processing moves the wave of completed calculations forward one step.

Once this loop is complete and the tip of this wave reaches the bottom-right of our matrix, the first phase of the calculation is complete. Most importantly, it was completed in x+y cycles rather than x*y cycles. While the test samples are too small to take accurate readings (1ms resolution in most browsers), the `animals` sample went from 10ms to under a millisecond. In contrast, the `lorem` sample went from 5.5 seconds to about 1 millisecond; no initial readings were taken for `identical`, `longchain`, or `gilbertsulivan` [webgl:477].

Even accounting for significant measurement errors, this is a considerable improvement!

We can see a significant improvement in speed in just the first 30 seconds of processing.

Conclusion

Some of this feels like a dirty hack; for example, working around all the references to RGBA feels weird. WebGL was designed for graphics, not computation. For the adventurous, this lends a sense of excitement and challenge.

This takes me back to my (very brief) days of working in `C`, where memory manipulation is a little closer at hand. Conforming to `vec4` memory (`rgba`) really encourages you to think of new ways of using (and abusing) the way you use memory, reusing memory, or squeezing that extra bit of information into an incompletely used byte (most of which has been refactored out of the example).

While I have loved Conway's Game of Life for decades, I never thought I would find a practical purpose for cellular automatons. Having noticed the similarity between this problem and GoL, I now want to revisit implementations of aerosolized particulate dispersion models.[24]

Lastly, the most educational part for me was the value of pencil and grid paper. A lot of debugging revolved around solving the grid with a pencil and comparing the resulting manually solved matrix to the program's solution.

Solving Smith-Waterman's by hand is also like doing a giant Sudoku or Crossword... kind of fun.

Next Steps

1. Open in the browser

---

[24]Smoke.js is an example of a dispersion model. https://omrelli.ug/smoke.js/

2. Hit **F12**

3. Insert a Break-point

4. Start stepping through the code

In this case, I suggest saving a local copy first to allow you to make minor changes to see the effect.

The performance gains I see by implementing the algorithm on the GPU were significant: approximately 5000 times in terms of speed. However, the more I ponder the problem, the more ways I see to improve it.

On the other hand ...

This tool was written as a personal utility to meet individual needs. Until there is more interest in M.I.S.S[25], there is likely little reason to implement performance gains.

It's fast enough... for now.

Looping

I suspect my calling of run in a loop is inefficient. Implementing the loop as part of the GPU code would likely be better. However, there are two reasons I did not do this:

1. The current implementation allows for periodic data reading and progress bars in the visualization (orange connectors).

---

[25]Measure of Similarity of Software of Students: An in browser code comparison utility
https://jefferey-cave.gitlab.io/miss/

2. Input and Output memory is declared before execution. In the helper functions, input and output memory are swapped after every run. I don't know how to do this within the context of a single execution.

Neither of these issues seem insurmountable.

Chain Resolution

Smith-Waterman calls for two phases

1. Build the chains

2. Resolve the chains

This article intentionally ignores the second phase of a Smith-Waterman, the code that reads the chains back off the memory. The current implementation in M.I.S.S. uses pure CPU JavaScript to resolve the chains. However, a recent discussion in the office made me rethink how that was done and inspired me to rewrite the chain resolution function to use the GPU more.

 I encourage readers to look at the GPU function chain [webgl.html:588-685] to see its implementation. It uses very similar techniques to those already discussed.

Memory Consumption

Building a 2-D matrix in memory means `height` **times** `width`. That is going to grow quickly, depending on your input. Also, as the number of tokens grows, there is a risk that the numbers representing them will exceed 65535 (2 bytes).

One of the initial validation tests was to compare the genomes of E.Coli[26] and Y.Pestarius[27] (available in the M.I.S.S samples as "bigcompare.zip"). Unfortunately, that eats up memory, and an 8TB array exceeds my laptop's capabilities.

I would love an implementation that cuts the giant matrix into a series of smaller 'tiles' (16000x16000 for about 2GB?). This would ensure they never consume more memory than is available and never generate a token identifier greater than 2 bytes.

Tokens could be mapped to an index not exceeding `UInt16` for the given tile. The tiles could be solved independently (in parallel if you have more than one GPU), storing only their internal chains and edges. The edges could then be stitched together during chain-resolution.

It's an interesting idea, and I'd love to see someone run with it...

Further Reading

Unfortunately, most of this was done as a personal project almost 2 years ago, so many of the references and tutorials I used have been lost to the mists of time (mists of time is about 20 minutes, in my case)

---

[26] National Library of Medicine, Escherichia coli LF82 chromosome, GenBank: CU651637.1
https://www.ncbi.nlm.nih.gov/nuccore/CU651637.1?report=fasta

[27] National Library of Medicine, Yersinia pestis KIM10+, GenBank: AE009952.1
https://www.ncbi.nlm.nih.gov/nuccore/AE009952.1?report=fasta

The Helper Functions

If you want to expand on this, I recommend investigating my helper functions. There is a lot of "stuff" going on.

Smith-Waterman

Unfortunately (or fortunately), my efforts to port and my lack of understanding resulted in a mash of non-functional code. The efforts to debug created my understanding but resulted in something that looked nothing like what was started with.

 GitHub: CheckSims

Much of my learning comes from simply stepping through the code samples given on Wikipedia and working through my own examples.

 Wikipedia: Smith-Waterman

 Wikipedia: Conway's Game of Life

Understanding the algorithms came by writing code in PoJS (Plain old JavaScript) without adding the complexity of a GPU. Now that I know GPUs better, I think it would have been the more straightforward solution... hindsight is 20/20, so who knows?

WebGL

 WebGL Fundamentals: was the primary set of tutorials I followed to figure out how to do things with WebGL

 Mozilla Developer Network: This is the defacto-standard reference for browser-related things and includes both tutorials and generic references for WebGL.

Libraries

WebGL is relatively new, and WebCL[28] (Web Computational Language) is still a work in progress. Fortunately, several libraries have been developed to make WebGL more computationally friendly.

 tensorflow.js: Google's famous library for machine learning... implemented in JavaScript

---

[28] WebCL Overview, Kronos Group
https://www.khronos.org/webcl/

TWGL: psGPU was meant to turn into what TWGL is. If I were to solve this problem again, I would use this library.

Avoiding Psychic Software Development

A tribute to James Randi for dummy programmers

- Inspired by Randi's skepticism, let us use critical thinking in software development

- Skepticism towards claims of task completion in software development and promises of quick fixes are emphasized.

- Popoff's exploitation of faith and the ADE-651's ineffective technology showcase the dangers of blind belief.

- Randi's legacy prompts reflection on the importance of evidence-based decision-making and skepticism in the face of extraordinary claims.

The Amazing Randi was a successful stage magician, famously surpassing many of Harry Houdini's achievements. Later in his career, James Randi took his mastery of magic and used it to turn a critical and skeptical eye to claims of paranormal powers. Claims of divine healing powers, telekinesis, and psychic powers were all put to the test with what grew to a $1,000,000 reward to anyone who could prove their powers.

The Randi Prize was <u>never claimed</u> during its 50 years.[29]

Modern Product Development

Edward Deming once said,

> In God we trust, all others must bring data.

Over my career I have become infamous for citing Deming, but if this is a time for confessions, I must confess that my knowledge of Deming came much later than my attitudes toward evidence based decision making. Rather, I can attribute my personal distrust of claims and constant demands for evidence to people like James Randi showing me how, and when, to be critical of my own beliefs.

Both Deming and Randi demand that we approach our observations critically and skeptically manage our own biases.

---

[29] James Randi Educational Foundation
https://web.randi.org/home/jref-status

This has impacted me professionally in two significant ways:

1. I am suspicious of software developers that claim they have finished a difficult task

2. I am suspicious of consultants promising to make problems go away quickly and cheaply

I say this as someone who has both development and consulting in his past.

A Personal Confession

In my youth, I was fascinated by psychic powers. I bought all the books on remote viewing, developing my psychic powers, and becoming a medium. I recognised that information was a powerful tool and was interested in any means to acquire more of it.

The problem is that, like Fox Mulder (X-Files), I've always wanted to believe. Lewellyn publishing can account for much of my allowance.

Unfortunately for my desire to believe, at some point I saw the now classic episode of What's My Line with guests James Hydric and James Randi.[30] In the show, Randi is skeptical and flat out states that Hydric's telekinetic ability to turn book pages amounts to him blowing on the pages,

---

[30] Classic Hoax: Psychic James Hydrick
https://wafflesatnoon.com/james-hydrick-psychic/

and introduces some light weight Styrofoam around the book. He is firm and calm, and completely unrelenting in his stance, and the scene eventually gets uncomfortably awkward as Hydric begins a convoluted explanation of his ensuing failures.

Hydric is a bit of a tragic character. While he was obviously a fraud, it appears he became so as an attention seeking behaviour. Watching his confessional interviews after the Randi event, I got the impression that he had come to believe his own hype; that he had misled even himself.

Whatever the case, Randi's critical approach to assessing paranormal capabilities has haunted my ability to blindly believe with a shadow of skepticism.

Software Developers

In the process of developing software, developers are expected to produce solutions to problems that have not been solved. That is the nature of the craft. However there are corporate expectations that the problem be solved in a reasonable amount of time, because time is money. This places pressure on developers to be finished, and this creates the risk space: scared for our job, eager to please, wanting to appear skilled, we **want** it to be done too.

So we tell our managers that the job is complete.

We are physically incapable of seeing that it does not completely solve the problem, or that it is too difficult to use in its current state. Like those that are healed by Faith, we want it to be true.

This is where processes and philosophies around the SDLC come into play.

- Issue boards keep us from reporting more progress than we have actually achieved

- Sprints and backlogs keep us focused on the most pressing issues

- Automated software build/test/deploy (CI/CD) ensures that evaluation is unbiased and reproducible.

While the debates continue about which controls are the best, there is no doubt that we need the controls. Like James Randi placing Styrofoam around a phone book, these controls ensure we are being honest ... even to ourselves.

Faith Healing

Even assuming it had been real, Hydric's ability to turn phone book pages was little more than a novelty act. It may have sold a few books, but debunking it was not exactly an earth-shattering revelation. A more significant case can be found in that of Peter Popoff.

Peter Popoff is an evangelical minister whose television broadcast became famous for his claims of divine knowledge and healing abilities. During his shows he would call arbitrary individuals from the audience by name and cite details of their life with no prior knowledge. As he approached them, and they began to stand, he would tell the gathered audience what terrible diseases the person had and that he would heal them. Both the knowledge and the healing were claimed to be directly imparted divine powers.

Rather than being divinely inspired, Randi discovered that Popoff's wife was the true source of knowledge. Prior to the show, she would gather information from attendees and was broadcasting their names and information via radio to an ear-piece he wore.

Here lies a case of fraud that demonstrates true harm.

People that sought out Popoff truly believed God spoke to him, and that his hands could remove illness from them. Believing that they had been cured meant that they would stop seeking treatment for arthritis, or epilepsy, or heart conditions. When one adds the $4 million a year in donations people made, Popoff has made it a little more difficult to replace the pills he told them to throw out.

James Randi, did thousands of people a service when he exposed Popoff. Though we do need to ask why Popoff continues his healing to this day.

Consultants and Vendors

One way management can reduce costs is to hire outside expert consultants that understand the problem better than the internal staff, and nobody knows the solutions better than the vendors. Naturally, as experts they are to be paid more than internal staff, this is justified by their being more knowledgeable.

Unfortunately, this is *often* not the case.

Due to the short time frame they are present for, consultants are not actually paid for measurable results. The measurable results of their suggestions and changes come after they have left. Their real rewards are tied to making the manager that hired them feel good about their decision. This does not necessarily mean they were successful at solving the problem.

Like the Faith Healer, consultants can reap huge rewards for making promises of solving problems, and making their audience feel that the problem has been solved through some special conference from an authority. Unfortunately, like the Faith Healer, this can be, and often is, done as an act of faith.

In fact, it is almost impossible for this to be *undone* because the person that has paid out their life savings to be healed, or the manager that has spent a significant portion of their budget, cannot admit to themselves that they were swindled.

> The more we pay, the more we *want to believe*.

I have worked with some great consultants over the years, but I've spent more working hours with bad ones. The reinforcement cycle is one in which the best rewards go to those who make management feel good. Unfortunately, they are also the ones that consume the most time in fixing and retrofitting good solutions around their popular one. Given they are paid by the hour, this means the feedback mechanism benefits the dishonest.

There is no easy answer to this except to be skeptical of smooth talking salesmen that echo what you already want to believe. Often consultants are brought in because local staff have been asked to solve a problem and have given an undesirable response. Unfortunately, that is often the honest, but hard-to-hear, truth.

Like James Randi upsetting a lot of Peter Popoff's believers, the truth can be hard to hear, but healthier for you in the long run.

Faith Healing in Modern Times

In reminiscing about the impact of James Randi, naturally I turned to Wikipedia to refresh my memory. It has been a long time since I have had need to know about Randi's work: a different time. We now rely on scientific reasoning, and no longer believe in psychics and faith healing. We no longer make business plans based on gut feelings but rather collect data to provide a basis for action.[31]

That was a different time, a simpler time.

Imagine my shock to learn that frauds Randi has exposed continue to be active as recently as 2015, with terrifying consequences.

According to Wikipedia, the ADE-651 is an explosive detection device that is used internationally to keep people safe from terrorism. Naturally, people want to be safe from terrorist bombs and put their faith in technological devices to protect them. Randi first challenged the developers of the device in 2008, and it has since been demonstrated to be ineffective, to the point of containing no operating machinery at all. The FBI has repeatedly issued bulletins to law enforcement to stop using the device. In spite of this, it continues to be used, as a life saving device,[32] by several countries and local law enforcement agencies.

---

[31] Data are not take for meuseum purposes, The Deming Institute https://deming.org/data-are-not-taken-for-museum-purposes -they-are-taken-as-a-basis-for-doing-something/

[32] SHC Dismisses Petition for Ban on 'Fake Bomb Detectors' https://propakistani.pk/2019/12/13/shc-dismisses-petition-seek ing-ban-on-fake-bomb-detectors-in-pakistan/

People are so desperate for it to be true, they just will not let it go, and people are dying as a result.

> The false sense of security provided by the device had catastrophic effects for many Iraqi people, hundreds of whom were killed in bombings that the ADE 651 failed to prevent
>
> — Wikipedia: ADE-651, Investigations, Iraq

Perhaps people cling to it for hope, perhaps they cling to it for vanity, but in these modern times, people are paying millions of dollars for devices that end up getting them killed.

Reading about the ADE-651 I am reminded that there is no quick cure for superstition. We still want to believe that we are finished, and still want to believe that we are clever, and we are still greedy when it comes to getting that promotion. Like Randi, all we can do is be eternally vigilant against our own fears, hopes, and biases.

Thank-you Mr. Randi

Randi has left a swath of fraudsters in his path: Uri Geller, James Hydric, Peter Popoff, James McCormick and many others. Each of them represents a swindler filling their pockets with millions by feeding on the hopes and fears of thousands of people. He showed the danger of blind faith, and importance of protecting ourselves from our own desires.

From time-to-time I still blame software errors on planetary alignment, or demonic possession. Other times I amaze people with my psychic ability to know an error without ever having to have seen the problem they are experiencing. But these are done in jest, and always followed by (at least the offer of) a detailed investigation or explanation as to how the discovery was made.

As individuals with a responsibility to achieve goals, and under pressure to deliver, its is sometimes hard to hold ourselves to account. Sometimes we feel tempted to give or accept false hope to preserve our own dignity. Randi's approach to debunking the paranormal did not make him friends with believers, but it cut directly to the heart of the matter. When lives[33] and livelihoods[34] are on the line[35] that's what really counts[36].

So thank-you, James Randi. You did not make friends among the frauds and charlatans of the world, but you certainly inspired at least one developer to push beyond the illusion of success.

---

[33] Boeing whistleblower alleges systemic problems with 737 MAX, The Seattle Times, 2020-06-18
https://www.seattletimes.com/business/boeing-aerospace/boeing-whistleblower-alleges-systemic-problems-with-737-max/

[34] Twitter breach exposes one of tech's biggest threats: Its own employees, NBC News, 2020-07-16
https://www.nbcnews.com/tech/security/twitter-breach-exposes-one-tech-s-biggest-threats-its-own-n1234076

[35] Breach at software provider to local governments, schools, ABC News, 2020-09-23
https://abcnews.go.com/Technology/wireStory/data-breach-software-provider-local-governments-73209257

[36] HSBC suffers IT outage, Information Age, 2017-02-27
https://www.information-age.com/hsbc-suffers-it-outage-4543/

Allow people to make assumptions and they will come away absolutely convinced that assumption was correct and that it represents fact ... It's not necessarily so.

Further Reading

This has been a personal tribute to a great man and some of the things he inspired me to think about, and the way he caused me to see the world. Naturally, as I was writing this, I came across some articles on perception and how, as humans, we want to be deceived.

New York Times: Sleights of Mind
An interesting discussion on the scientific description of how magic is based in cognitive perception

Skeptic News
Randi's recommended daily reading of skeptic news sources that approach the world with a critical and scientific eye

If you are impressed with James Randi, you should also learn about

Margaret Hamilton

who put quality control at the forefront of her teams software design, saving the Apollo Moon landing; but who's design of a error free programming language is largely forgotten

Edwards Deming

the father of data driven decision making

... and in the interest of being skeptical of Randi, and because I still want to believe

The Myth of James Randi's Million Dollar Challenge

an article critical of Randi's requirements for the prize, which indicates he may have used it as a vessel for suppressing legitimate evidence.

The Unbelievable Skepticism of James Randi

A slightly more critical look at Randi's life's work. Raises questions about Randi's personal bias and profit motive.

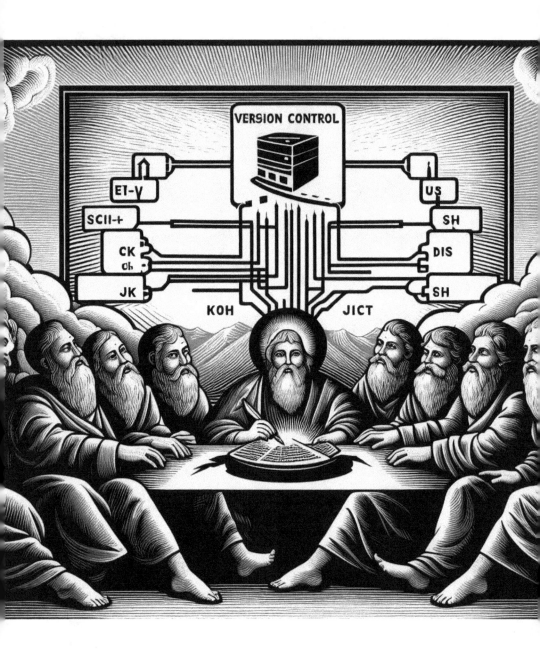

Git and the Intermittent Network

A personal experience with network failure

- Benefits and risks associated with modern digital platforms; Emphasis on availability, sustainability, and growth capability.

- Reflection on the historical development of the Internet.

- Evolution of version control systems like Git and SVN to enable offline work

Within my organization, we have been moving toward modern web-based platforms. These offer many benefits to our users regarding availability, sustainability, and growth capability, and I have been one of their leading proponents.

While modern web-based services are the norm and desirable, their risks should be considered for mitigation. These risks revolve around the centralisation of service and the network availability of clients. These risks are well understood, and most tools used by modern development teams were designed with these types of issues in mind. However, as the Internet becomes more pervasive and stable, we commonly lose sight of its limitations.

A Personal Experience

As I write this, I am experiencing an internet outage.

This event occurred mid-meeting and has resulted in a situation where I cannot connect to the online resources required to complete my corporate objectives:

1. No connection to a production server to conduct repairs on that server (or even inspect the logs)

2. No connection to Microsoft Azure to conduct experimental work in our laboratory environment

3. All forms of meeting communications have been cut off (MS Teams, Webex, VOIP telephone)

4. An Outlook plugin cannot connect to an encryption server and is frozen because it is attempting to show me an encrypted email.

5. I can't take any corporate training I'm supposed to do or read that manual for that new tool I'm investigating.

I'm completely dead in the water.

According to my provider, a fibre-optic line has been cut somewhere between Halifax and Montreal resulting in massive connectivity loss for the region. The only productive task left to me is to write up an assessment of the current failure, on my local device, and upload it to the network when communication is re-established.

Hold on... Did I just describe getting work done and loading it later? That is a well-known caching strategy for resolving network latency issues.

Historical Note

The Internet, as we understand it, has not always been as accessible, available, or reliable as we have come to expect.

It is worth remembering that The Internet was initially designed as a distributed communication tool to allow the military to continue operating remote computers in the event of massive node loss (dating back to 1966). The assumption of loss of network availability has been an underlying assumption of much of the Internet's growth and is built into its fabric.

In the early days of general access to internet services, connections to the network were made intermittently. This was performed by dial-up connections, which would be initiated for short periods.

As networks became more common and robust, much of the shared development of software (open source) began to be shared across the network, as opposed to letter carriers and print (via the Share catalogue). Unfortunately, internationally, not all network connections are created equally, and some users suffered from several disruptions to connectivity.

What was Share?

In the mid-1950s, a user organisation for scientific applications ... was formed. One of its most important functions was serving as a clearinghouse for contributed software subroutines. The organisation was called Share ... and the contributed routines became the first library of reusable software.

— Robert L. Glass, Facts and Fallacies of Software Engineering

---

Out of this sense of sharing evolved several clearing houses such as SourceForge, Tigris, and eventually GitLab and GitHub. Unfortunately, even these clearing houses were subject to disruption.

In the highly competitive days just after Y2K, several organizations rose and fell rapidly and crises formed when code hosting platforms were simply turned off due to corporate takeover, sabotage, copyright infringement lawsuits, or even simple bankruptcy. Thousands of hours of work were lost to the simple issue of the centralized servers being turned off. Modern VCS (Version Control System) solutions (such as Git) evolved in this environment, allowing each node to retain complete histories of work and projects through a single surviving distributed node.

In recent years, <u>CAP theorem</u> has evolved to explain that high availability comes at certain costs, which, once the costs are accepted, can offer the benefits seen by the BBC newspaper during the Russo-Georgian conflict. During this period, communication lines were severed, meaning that correspondents and readers could not communicate across national boundaries. Service continued to be delivered to each side of the boundary, allowing reporters to continue reporting and commenters to continue to offer feedback during the entire conflict. Automated synchronization of news reports and on-the-ground reader comments occurred when alternate communication paths were established.

Each of these historic scenarios have common elements:

- contributors are forced to disconnect from communication and wait

- contributors wish to continue to prepare their communications

- caching is used to overcome communication latency, allowing people to continue working locally until the connection is reestablished.

This batching, or caching, can mitigate connectivity issues with web development platforms.

Web Based Publishing

Despite published content, content development has many common elements throughout its progression. Whether this is the dynamic content of software or the static content of News Videos, there is a common process for creating and distributing the content online.

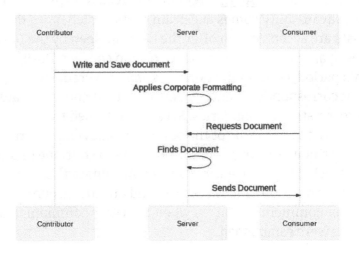

To use the example of an individual publishing an article to their newspaper (maybe their blog), they (the `Contributor`) would connect to the Internet (`NetProviderA`) and type their article into Open Journal Service, WordPress, or Medium (the `Server`). They can continue typing into the software on the Server, perhaps running spell and grammar checks until they hit the publish button. At this point, the consumer can retrieve the message whenever the customer wants.

The software development process would be the same as that of web-based development tools. The contributor would connect to the Internet, edit their document on the server, and indicate readiness to publish, making the application available to consumers.

Intermittent Connections

Looking at the historical development of the Internet and the current issue, we can see a risk associated with the network's not being available. We cannot consider the server in isolation and must include the network's effects.

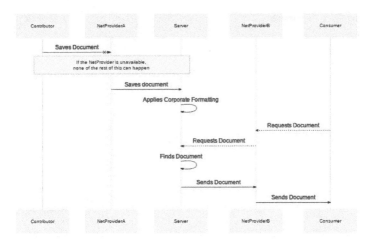

If the contributor's network connection is terminated, they cannot perform **any** work. Sticking to the newspaper article example, the author may have an excellent idea in mind, know of a flaw in the argument, or (frankly) want to get some work toward the publishing deadline; unfortunately, they are stopped.

Another layer that can be considered to overcome this issue is the local computer, which can be used to cache work: the contributor can type their document on their local computer and save it to their local disk.

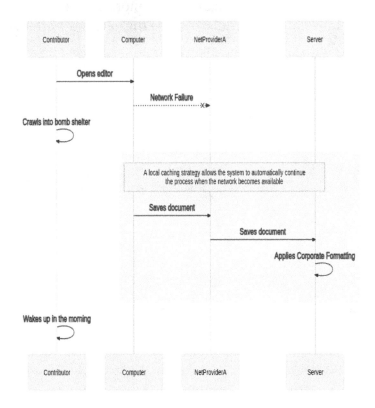

Looking at the previously discussed internet history, we can look to VCS tools to assist us in solving this problem. SVN and Git (as well as their predecessors and competitors) were developed in an environment where work needed to be buffered against future connections. Specifically, work needs to be performed and stored locally until it is possible to transmit it.

This has been an ongoing evolution, and Linus Torvalds specifically developed Git to resolve buffering issues he saw in SVN.

This has been an ongoing evolution, and Linus Torvalds specifically developed Git to resolve buffering issues he saw in SVN.

Local or Web

Using local development tools and synchronizing periodic changes is a common practice that allows us to communicate only the changes we are committed to. Still, this practice also offers the benefit of resolving latency issues. During 2020, lockdowns have resulted in many of us having to work from home and being remotely positioned in our workspace. We are using networks established for scenarios that demand significantly less resilience (binge-watching movies) and situations that require significant resilience (earning income to pay for groceries). This can be surprising for those of us whose livelihoods have become tied to these networks for the first time. In cases where the Internet has temporarily failed, and we are left unable to progress, it can be distressing to our managers and ourselves.

This does not mean that local tools are better than web-based tools.

For many years, my favourite platform was Cloud9, an online web-based IDE that allowed workstations to be set up on demand. This allowed me to maintain several development environments that met various needs. The ability to pick up work from anywhere in the world allowed me to continue working on projects from a hotel courtyard in Ecuador, from an old, indestructible RCA Cambios. The ability of the vendor to supply me with a powerful remote computer meant I could work from a $100 computer. This means I received software upgrades immediately and could work from any cheap hardware I could scrounge up.

There are trade-offs to consider, and that is what this has been about. Be aware of the trade-offs before wholly committing to one solution or the other. IDE vendors want you to be tied to their tool, and this reduces many of the benefits of distributed VCS platforms. On the other hand, we have computing networks; take advantage of them.

Ultimately, I recommend a balanced approach that takes lessons from the Internet's rich history of information sharing.

Use Web-based IDEs, but use generic ones. Do not depend on always having access to the vendor's editor. Instead, maintain regular local pulls from your VCS repository and use programming languages and data formats based on simple text. This allows you to switch to a local copy during network outages and protects you from vendor lock-in.

Further Reading

As ever, Wikipedia has become the place to start. I recommend reading the article on <u>Version Control Systems</u>.

There are several generic, web-based IDEs that I have enjoyed using:

- <u>Theia</u> (Eclipse Foundation)

- <u>Eclipse Che</u> (Eclipse Foundation)

- <u>Cloud9</u> (Amazon)

- <u>GitPod</u> (Git Pod)

Interestingly, each can be served on your corporate network (to protect your institution's intellectual property) or installed on your local computer, allowing you to continue working when your network gets nuked, or a ship's anchor snags your data cable.

Somebody, please take my money

The business of software. A guide for dummy programmers

- A major retailer could not find a way to make a sale despite a willing customer.

- This highlights systemic issues in the software and information system industry.

- Historic examples and modern methodologies of quality assurance in digital systems

- Programmers, managers, and executives must prioritize functionality and quality over superficial features.

I spent 6 hours today trying to buy a printer ... and failed.

- There is money set aside for this purchase in my bank account.

- There are printers on the shelves

- Websites advertise printers for sale

I could not purchase a printer because a corporation with a near monopoly on the Canadian market, one of Canada's largest privately owned retailers, could not tell me *which printers they had available for sale.*

Let that sink in:

A multi-billion dollar retailer could not tell me if they had anything to sell me.

On the surface, this is laughable and funny, but it belies a more insidious, pervasive, and downright dangerous problem.

The Sequence of Events

I recently made a long-distance move across almost the entirety of Canada. I'll credit the movers; most of my stuff made it across in one piece; unfortunately, my printer suffered catastrophic snapping of some hinges. Since we do not deal in paper as much as we used to, my wife and I initially just tried to live without it; in the short term, this saved us a bunch of money, but it also helped us to evaluate what we really needed in a printer:

1. Scanner with an auto-feeder

2. Cheaper ink cartridges

3. Duplex printing (nice to have)

4. Ink colours in separate cartridges (nice to have)

After a moment of distress trying to print a government form, and with a reasonably clear idea of what I wanted, my Wife and I decided to end the problems and pick something (anything) up at a nearby retailer: Staples Canada.

Naturally, my first reaction was to look on their website: staples.ca. Reviewing a listing of available products over a cup of coffee in our pyjamas was exactly the way to start figuring out what we wanted. It was a quick search:

- all available printers

- ordered by price

Jumping to the first couple of printers that met our needs would give us a good idea of our critical price point. Further, I also saw they had an option for 2-hour curbside pickup, so we should be picking it up in a couple of hours. We found a couple of printers, at around $100, that met our needs. Within 30 minutes, we clicked to order.

- None available in-store

- None available online

What? That's annoying. Let's try the next one.

- None available in-store

- None available online

Hold up. Let's try a filter: Only show items with 2-hour delivery. Surely, that will filter to items available in the store **right now**.

- None available in-store

- None available online

The more I searched, the more frustrated I became. After an hour, my wife and I finally decided to go into the store and buy whatever they had available.

Upon arriving at the store, it didn't take long for us to narrow in on the products we were looking for. They were more expensive than their equivalents online, but they were there.

... or were they?

We narrowed it down to one of three printers when a clerk arrived. We pointed to them and asked a couple of questions, and he stated: well, we should probably check to see if they are available before we go any further. They may not have them in stock.

Momentarily slack-jawed, we proceeded for him to check to see if they were in stock, only to find that they weren't.

None of the printers we had expressed an interest in were available for purchase. They were on the shelf, but none of them were available for sale. The clerk suggested we go online to check availability.

None of the printers we had expressed an interest in were available for purchase. They were on the shelf, but none were available for sale. The clerk suggested we go online to check availability.

As we left the store empty-handed, the manager stopped us and asked if we had found everything we were looking for (no) and how he could help. He spent the next two hours explaining that it wasn't his fault they had no stock and trying to upsell me a high-performance Laser Printer. My only question at this point is: Is it available for purchase?

The manager gave me a customer complaint phone number and promised to email me a link to a printer I was interested in. He had verified with the warehouse that it was available, and I could get it shipped to the store. He could not request it, but there should be no difficulty if I ordered it online via the website.

$\times$ In-store Pick up not available at

The results of my attempt to order a Brother MFC-J497DW from Staples.ca

On my way home, I stopped at the local hardware store to pick up a ladder and a shovel. They didn't have any ladders in stock but pointed me to their website.

$\oslash$ Temporarily out of stock online.
View similar in-stock items

Clicking on the similar in-stock items link on HomeHardware.ca had no effect at all.

The Significance

These are fundamental problems in the Software and Data Systems space: inventory systems should be able to count inventory, and sales systems should be able to sell products. Businesses are allowing systems to be released without testing the requested fundamental feature, which is a massive failure. Software developers are allowing the release of features that do not work... and not in subtle, nuanced ways.

It's like manufacturing a car and forgetting to attach one of the wheels.

Information systems are just that: systems. They integrate humans and information to achieve a goal. In this case, the business itself is its inventory management processes, and they were completely nonfunctional across multiple paths to success.

1. No validation of the system had taken place

2. No alternatives for success were planned for

That is fairly significant, and I suspect there are two elements at play:

1. The development was outsourced to a consulting firm that is motivated to appease managers.

2. It is highly likely that the feature was delivered on schedule.

Software development has been commoditized, and in the process, the managers and developers have forgotten a fundamental truth: software is built to solve real-world problems that real people have. If you develop tools that don't work, people are hurt. Even if it is just because they have to manually search through a store's catalogue or because they have to add up numbers in a spreadsheet before entering into the payroll system, they are still hurt. While it is up to developers to **enact** that quality, managers must **expect** quality.

This means deadlines may not be met.

... but then again, you have to ask if the feature isn't implemented, has the deadline been met?

It's Embarrassing

Since the dawn of software development, testing and validation of the work has been paramount. When you entrust a person to design a process to take care of people, it must take care of people. Human judgment is no longer involved to cover your mistakes in process design: if your process is flawed, the machine will carry out a flawed process.

Margaret Hamilton realized this in the '60s when her team developed the software that landed the Apollo, introducing the concept of Software Engineer. She did not develop software that worked because astronauts are trained not to make mistakes but because she tested the crap out of her software. Later, this led to the <u>languages 001 and USL</u>, which made process designers think about errors before they happened ... because that's what programmers do.

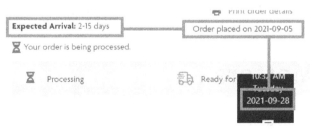

After 23 days, Home Hardware was unable to tell me anything more than my order is in progress. After asking me if I'd like to wait it out, we took another 10 minutes and cancelled the order.

In the late 1990s and early 2000s, unit testing, test-driven development, continuous integration, and automated regression testing came into their own, offering means of ensuring that features were guaranteed to be *minimally* tested for basic user expectations prior to release.

 DevOps in 2010 should have made developers even more responsible for basic functionality testing, making them directly answerable for the system's errors.

The issue is likely two-fold:

1. Managers believe the skill lies in the visual elements they can see rather than the business processes they cannot.

2. Developers are not standing up for the engineering act they are engaged in.

It was a very long time and a lot of hard work before Hamilton's peers considered software a type of engineering. Watching software be released that does not meet the most basic functionality requirements makes me realize that many developers need to live up to her legacy. I'll take it one step further ... managers must stop expecting software to have the "testing" check-box tick and start understanding that quality is a continuous improvement mindset.

It Matters

I raise this as a moment of reflection within Information Systems and Software Engineering.

Airplanes are <u>falling out of the sky</u>

 Small business owners are being <u>falsely accused and imprisoned</u>

 Young mothers have their <u>children taken from them</u>

... and ... Retail organizations are physically <u>unable to sell their products</u>

Programmers need to consider the direct consequences of their actions; Managers need to take a moment and reflect on the value they are adding to their organization; and Executives need to reconsider the actual deliverables they are asking for.

Turn a Shiny Dashboard into a Desktop App

Because sometimes bureaucracy gets in the way

- Learn how to deploy a Shiny dashboard as a desktop app, sidestepping the hurdles of server deployment and organizational red tape.

- Create a seamless user experience with a starter script that loads the application from a shortcut, minimizing the need for technical expertise.

- Explore how this approach extends beyond Shiny, enabling the deployment of various web-based applications that offer flexibility and ease of access in diverse organizational environments.

Sample Code available on GitLab

Jeff Cave / shinyapp-desktop · GitLab

Shiny is a popular web publishing service, unfortunately, not every application can be deployed on servers. This tutorial demonstrates a simple means by which to deploy a shiny app to desktop by creating a Site Specific Browser. Mostly to skip the bureaucratic begging for a server.

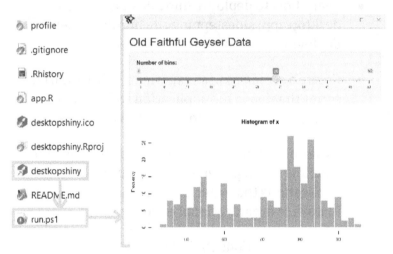

An R-Shiny dashboard can be run as a desktop application, from a double click, to give non-technical users a seamless experience.

Once upon a time, one of the Data Scientists in our organization called me with a problem. They had spent significant time putting together a dashboard in R and Shiny and wanted to know where they could host it to share it with clients.

They wanted to know where our Shiny server was stored and how they could publish to it.

It took everything I had not to laugh at them.

The thing I was working on when he called was a generic deployment system for precisely that kind of project.

However, I was running into negotiations with Security, Finance, and Architecture ... everybody has to have their say. To get him the server he wanted, I estimated years.

Like any large organization, the bureaucracy must be fed.

This was a massive blow to the Data Scientist. His team had been developing the dashboard for months. The business had invested precious effort in describing its informational needs. The team had demonstrated the value of Shiny. They were ready to realize all that effort, and the organization's statement was: We can't do that.

That's a lot of wasted effort.

After some discussion, I took pity on him and his team (and myself; I'd actually invested a lot of my coffee breaks coaching his junior Data Scientists).

- Your customer's need the dashboard now? (yes)

- Is the dashboard computationally expensive? (no)

- Do you have a shared folder in which you could publish the application? (yes)

- Are the customers at all technically savvy? (no)

I told him to give me the weekend, and I'd give him a prototype solution on Monday.

Project

The intent is not to teach how to do complex mathematics or write Shiny Apps but to demonstrate how to configure a project within the organizational environment. Hopefully, this will act as a springboard, helping users set up quickly.

The code itself is a simple demo app exported from RStudio. The real trick is to get it to run on the desktop environment.

The expectation is that the developer wants to deploy a shared application but is in an environment with no Shiny server, and there is not likely to be one anytime soon. Rather than wait, the developer can take advantage of a shared folder structure and an <u>old feature of Firefox</u> to run the application on individual desktops. While not as elegant, this solution represents a solution that is likely suitable for most reporting needs and can be implemented immediately (using the tools already present).

Pre-Requisites

- Windows

- RStudio

- Rscript

- Git

- Firefox

The demo assumes you have RStudio installed and will interact with the system via PowerShell. There is no reason this will not work on Linux; however, it is not what we use at the office, so it was not tested on it.

Checkout the base project

To get started, clone the sample project and open it in RStudio

1. Navigate:
   https://gitlab.com/jefferey-cave/shinyapp-desktop

2. Click: Fork

3. Open your copy of the project

4. Get the clone URL

5. Go to the command line and checkout the project

```
cd ~/Project/Folder;
git clone
https://gitlab.com/jefferey-cave/shinyapp-desktop.git;
cd shinyapp-desktop;
ls -al;
```

You should see a listing of all the files in the project.

Before we proceed, we should check to see if the project runs on our computer. This ensures no basic configuration issues before the actual work begins.

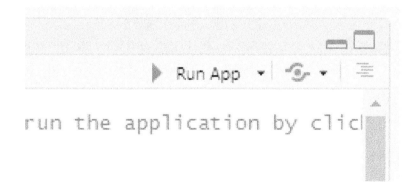

1. Double-click on the file desktopshiny.Rproj

2. Open: app.R

3. Click: Run App

You should see the shiny app open in the built-in browser, though, depending on your environment, you may have to resolve some dependencies.

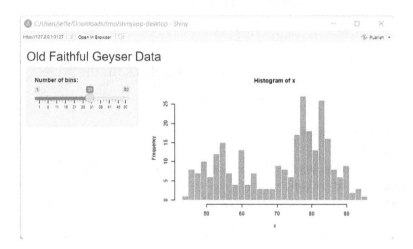

Proof that the application is running and any problems we may experience are not with the computer configuration or app code.

Create a Starter Script

While knowing the application works is nice, it could be a better user experience. We have been asked to create an app for those less technically inclined, and they should not need an instruction manual to get up and running.

We can ease their experience by creating a starter script that loads their application from a shortcut.

The first thing to note is the output during the run of our Shiny dashboard. When we click on the button **Run App** we see the exact **R** command being executed to achieve all of this and its output:

```
shiny::runApp()
Listening on http://127.0.0.1:5436
```

Try copying/pasting your URL into your local browser; you should see the same app.

Knowing that there is an R command that will start our application, we can skip the IDE and run the application using rscript

1. Stop your app in RStudio

2. Open a PowerShell terminal

3. Change to your project folder

4. Run your project using rscript

```
rscript.exe -e "shiny::runApp('.')"
```

Your app should be started, but without having to have the customer load the IDE:

```
Listening on http://127.0.0.1:3145
```

Try pointing your browser at that new URL. You should be looking at the app.

> **NOTE**
>
> The port changes every time you start. It is
> randomly assigned at start-time. You can specify
> the port that will be used; however, if we put
> together more than one dashboard, having a
> random port means less coordination between data
> scientists (it should just work).
>
> We will not make assumptions about the start
> conditions or set a static port.

If we check the `runApp` parameters, there is one extra
parameter we can include to make this a little more
user-friendly:

```
rscript.exe -e "shiny::runApp('.',launch.browser=TRUE)"
```

Save that in a text file called `start.ps1`.

You now have a basic script for users to start your
interactive report. Having your customers click on the
`start` script will give them a (mostly) seamless
experience.

Creating a new browser instance

Since Shiny advertises the port it is listening on, we can
capture that information and then instantiate a *special
browser instance* on behalf of the user.

For our users, we could start a browser instance *just for the application*. We also want to stop the Shiny instance when the browser stops using it.

> There is no data. There is only XUL!
>
> (the XUL platform slogan)

For this example, we will use Firefox, which is based on the XUL platform and has a well-documented and modifiable interface. To summarize (in a brutal way), Firefox is a webpage that can be dynamically modified (if you know how). We are going to use this feature to create a primitive <u>Site-Specific Browser</u>.

We can extend our shiny server starting script using PowerShell to listen for the advertised port. We can then use this advertised URL and port to start a Firefox instance.

```powershell
# Start `rscript` and capture `stderr` for the port number
& "rscript.exe" -e "shiny::runApp('.')" 2>&1 |
  % {
    # look for the `url` line
    if($_ -like '*Listening on*'){
      # Parse the input for the url
      ("$_" -replace ".*Listening on ",'').Trim();
    }
  } |
  % {
    # open FireFox using the discovered URL
    & "C:\Program Files\Firefox\firefox.exe" $_
  };
```

This solution gets us part way there: we are starting a unique browser instance for the shiny app.

The issue is that when we terminate our Firefox instance, our Shiny instance continues to run in the background. We must manually stop it.

We can continue to modify our script to start both the Shiny dashboard and the Firefox instance separately, then allow our script to maintain enough intelligence about them to monitor their independent process states.

```
# Start the `shiny` "thread"
$shiny = Start-Job -Name "shiny" -ArgumentList($pwd)
-ScriptBlock{
  param($workingdir);
  cd $workingdir;

# Start the shiny app and print the URL

  & "rscript.exe" -e "shiny::runApp('.')" 2>&1 | % {
    if($_ -like '*Listening on*'){
      ("$_" -replace ".*Listening on ",'').Trim()
    }
  }
}
```

At this point, Shiny is started as a `job`, and $shiny maintains a reference that can then be used to stop the job later. This does add the problem that we need to read from the output stream slightly differently.

```
#poll the shiny thread for output
while ($shiny.HasMoreData -or $shiny.State -eq "Running") {
```

```
  $url = $shiny.ChildJobs[0].output.readall();
  # when we find the URL ... stop
  if($url){
    break;
  }
}
```

Now, we have the URL at the script level and can proceed to start Firefox.

Again, we want to create a separate process that we can monitor.

```
# create an array of arguments
$args = @('-profile','./profile','-new-instance',"-url
`"$url`"");
# start the firefox instance
$ff = Start-Process "C:\Program Files\Firefox\firefox.exe"
-ArgumentList $args -PassThru -Wait
```

This will block the script until Firefox stops.

Pay close attention to the arguments passed to Firefox.

- **profile**: This uses a pre-existing profile that is customized to our purposes.

- **new-instance**: Ensures it does not re-use any instances of Firefox that may already be open

- **Wait**: Ensures that the PowerShell job blocks processing until it ($ff) completes

This forces a `new-instance`, a new `profile`, and a `wait` until Firefox completes. The custom profile is used to manipulate how Firefox appears to the user. For the adventurous, inspect the included profile to see ways you can manipulate Firefox to make it behave more like we want.

Our final step is to stop the shiny process once the Firefox process has terminated.

```
Stop-Job $shiny.Id
```

The completed script looks like this:

```
$shiny = Start-Job -Name "shiny" -ArgumentList($pwd)
-ScriptBlock{
  param($workingdir);
  cd $workingdir;
  & "rscript.exe" -e "shiny::runApp('.')" 2>&1 | % {
    if($_ -like '*Listening on*'){
      ("$_" -replace ".*Listening on ",'').Trim()
    }
  }
}


while ($shiny.HasMoreData -or $shiny.State -eq "Running") {
  $url = $shiny.ChildJobs[0].output.readall();
  if($url){
    break;
  }
}
$args = @('-profile','./profile','-new-instance',"-url
`"$url`"");
```

```
$ff = Start-Process "C:\Program Files\Firefox\firefox.exe"
-ArgumentList; $args -PassThru -Wait;
Stop-Job $shiny.Id;
```

You should be able to run the script.

```
.\run.ps1
```

and (eventually... it's a little slow) see your app running in
a window.

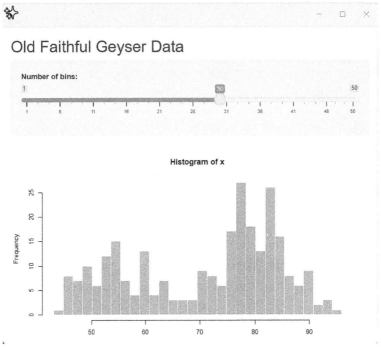

Our dashboard, running as a standalone desktop application. The icon
can be changed by modifying the files in the profile folder.

Creating a Shortcut

One of the issues with creating a PowerShell script is that regular users can't run it without a bit of know-how. The easiest way to get around this is to create an old fashioned **BAT** file.

```
cd <working directory>
C:\Windows\System32\WindowsPowerShell\v1.0\powershell.
exe ".\run.ps1"
```

Sure, Microsoft asked us to stop using that in 1995, but ... we are already in the depths of "get things done".

You will likely get an error if you run this as a regular user. The problem is that Windows (in their infinite wisdom) makes scripting unavailable to users by default. This is to protect them from malicious scripts.

To activate the script, you must indicate you know what you are doing. Since we only want our users to see the desktop window, we may as well hide the console window while we are at it.

```
cd <working directory>
C:\Windows\System32\WindowsPowerShell\v1.0\powershell.e
xe -windowstyle hidden -executionpolicy bypass
".\run.ps1"
```

- **executionpolicy**: allows the script to be run

- **`windowstyle`**: will enable us to hide the terminal window

Since this is a desktop application, a shortcut file (**LNK**) is better than the above **BAT** file. These allow us to specify all the same parameters and an icon file while removing all the console windows.

The link settings dialogue, showing it filled in and with the icon set

1. Navigate to the working directory in Windows Explorer

2. Right-Click > New ... > Shortcut

3. Set the properties

   ○ Target

```
C:\Windows\System32\WindowsPowerShel
l\v1.0\powershell.exe -windowstyle
hidden -executionpolicy bypass
".\run.ps1"
```

- o Start in

  `<working directory>`

- o `Change Icon ...`

By setting those three options, your users are a double click away from a reasonably seamless desktop experience.

A Happy(ish) Colleague

The lead for the Data Science team I was working with was (reasonably) happy with the solution. It was a hack, but it got his team up and running in a matter of days.

We both agreed that the optimal solution was to get a Shiny Server installed on-prem and link the URL from the internal website, so I put him in touch with the correct procurement experts and gave him this solution. I don't know what ever came of the procurement.

We refined the team's solution (mostly automating the deployment to the shared filesystem from GitLab's CI/CD features), but for the most part, the above solution represents a quick and dirty way for Data Scientists to get their work in front of data-driven decision makers.

To this day, the internal website maintains a link starting with `file:///` that points to the shared network file system.

For those paying attention, this solution is not constrained to Shiny but to any served web application: Node, Python, or perhaps something tucked away in a docker instance. This can also constrain a user to a web-based application to prevent students from cheating in a test or keep a temporary labour pool focused on their tasks.

I make no claims that this is the *right* solution; what I suggest is that it is *feasible*. Any organization that can build a Shiny application also has the tools to implement this solution. I share this solution, hoping it helps another Data Developer when Bureaucracy gets in the way.

130

How fast is fast enough?

A rambling discussion of the implications of Real-Time data

My claim: real-time is anything faster than a change can be observed

- **Understanding Real-Time Data**: "Real-time" means different things in different contexts, defined by the observer's ability to observe the change

- **Everyday Impacts**: Critically think about how fast information is required to make decisions.

- **Finding the Right Balance**: Explore practical examples of matching data processing speed with human needs.

Years ago, I got into a lunchtime discussion of real-time data processing, and a couple of guys at the table started in with a macho attitude:

1. I used to work on fighter jets ... real-time is microseconds

2. I used to do nuclear weapons testing ... real-time is nanoseconds

3. I used to do solar flare warning systems ...

As the time scale increasingly reduced, I realized that my perspective differed. I came from a healthcare setting that involved patient charts. In my head, inter-hospital patient transfers were the shortest timescale for transferring information, which involved humans reading and interpreting textual information. In this case, the information bottleneck was the time it would take for the patient to arrive at the new site and the staff at the new site to read the chart. (1-2 hours, sometimes up to a shift change)

One of the other developers at the table shared my slower perspective. In a previous lifetime, she had developed automated terrorism threat assessments and resource deployment systems (at least, this is true in my head ... she was always a little vague about what she had done previously). She was doing push notifications, but her bottleneck was the time it took for humans to comprehend the information they had received and to strap on a rifle. She put real-time at 15-30 minutes.

Timestamps

How we think about time is often built on a lifetime of assumptions.

In some database systems, there is a datatype known as a `timestamp`. A `timestamp` is a sequential number applied to the system. It is not a date or time but a point in time.

There is a very poignant scene in the TV show Angel in which Lorne (the karaoke hosting daemon) is counselling someone after a breakup: "I can hold a note for a long time ... But eventually, that's just noise. It's the change we're listening for ... That's what makes it music."

I have often extended this point: The change of state defines time; time itself is a perception of a changing state. This may be an oversimplification, but in terms of managing data, it is a useful one. From *our system's point of view*, there has been no change, and therefore, no time has passed. Our system perceives time differently than we do, so it is natural that it should use a different convention for recording time.

In terms of timestamps, we should have point-in-time 1, then point-in-time 2, followed by ...

Time is only observable at its smallest division; time's smallest division is the point of observed change.

Observation of change defines time. A point made most obvious by <u>Horse In Motion</u> and the <u>Zoopraxiscope</u> in 1880 (IMG: Wikimedia: CC-SA 2.5)

Real-time happens when change occurs between the observable points, so it is available at the next observation point (or possibly even creates the following observation).

Human Speed

In high school, a friend and I discovered <u>Network Time Protocol (NTP)</u>[37] and the <u>Canadian Atomic Clocks</u>[38]. While

---

[37] RFC–1305, Network Time Protocol (Version 3)
https://datatracker.ietf.org/doc/html/rfc1305
[38]

reading the user manual by the National Research Council, I remember reading the request to *not use the most accurate servers.*

It was just a friendly request to be polite.

The way the system works is that depending on how accurate your needs are, you are supposed to use a decreasingly reliable stratum of service. Stratum 1 sits right on top of the atomic clock, Stratum 2 servers update from Stratum 1 (introducing some potential error), and Stratum 3 servers update from Stratum 2 servers (introducing some more potential error). So, at the time, you were politely asked to use Stratum 3 servers to avoid overloading the Stratum 1 computers.

Seems fair.

Unfortunately, people are people, and my friend began updating his analogue watch (readable to the minute) by hand with Stratum 1 servers. When I told him Stratum three (accurate in the range of milliseconds) was good enough and that he was decreasing the accuracy for everyone, he boldly told me, "Nope, only Stratum 1 is accurate enough for me."

---

https://nrc.canada.ca/en/certifications-evaluations-standards/canadas-official-time

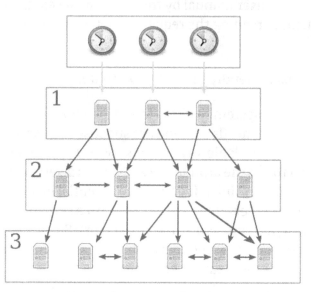

You are supposed to use the stratum of service appropriate to your needs. Stratum 1 sits right on top of the atomic clock, with each stratum reading from the previous level. (IMG: Wikimedia: Public Domain)

Macho statements aside, it is obvious that the speed bottleneck in the system is human-scale, not computer-scale, let alone atomic.

- A $10 watch will not retain accurate time for a long time. The drift in the network is less than the drift of the watch itself.

- An analogue interface, interacting with a human eye, is going to have a reading accuracy that is sub-minute, which is perfectly acceptable for the human turning the knob, who cannot achieve better than sub-minute accuracy anyway.

- The consumer is trying to promptly attend classes and meetups at the coffee shop. The time it takes to physically navigate the space between these events introduces variance at the sub-quarter-hour level.

Society does not function at the microseconds.

At the time, the norm was to leave approximately 15 minutes to account for the vagaries of life. This is consistent for two people suffering from 5 minutes of error: 10 minutes of error plus 5 minutes of agreement. 15 minutes was real-time.

My friend's effort to achieve a smaller resolution was a complete waste of time. At the same time, other people were genuinely being harmed.

- Data Scientists relying on accurate time for weather modelling are hurt.

- Sailors at sea, getting lousy weather predictions, are hurt.

- My friend gets hurt when everyone is annoyed at him for being late because he was fiddling with his watch to make it accurate.

Faster than Observed

I rarely see anyone reading data more frequently than daily. Even with push notifications, I receive a text message telling me to take action, but I'm happy if I can take action within a quarter business day.

Note

Faster is still better than slower; and real time is faster than the change can be observed.

In a business setting, an executive, manager, or business unit often calls for a monthly report on the 31st; weekly reports are run on Friday.

This is a huge mistake; we can do better given automated systems. Real-time is still something we can strive for, and a key benefit is that the results don't change significantly if we achieve faster than observable rates.

 Since 2010, I have had a trading bot developed in <u>Google Sheets and JavaScript</u>[39] (I'm cheap and love free computing power) that sends me a text message any time I need to make a trade. The fastest data I receive is 15-minute delayed price data, but the most significant data I receive is published quarterly (Financial Reports). This data must be aggregated into averages and deviations and ... patterns. The system is attempting to establish normal, and normal (by definition) doesn't change by much.

This is true for most human-scale systems most of the time.

Under these conditions, we are dealing with aggregate data. The changes are aggregated into averages over days, weeks, or even quarters. The assessments are not going to change significantly on an hourly basis. This means that the evaluation from yesterday is about the same assessment I will get today. I may see a change in the general trend, but it will be subtle and non-actionable in the short term.

There is a massively beneficial implication to this.

---

[39] Google Apps Script is a Javascript instance that runs in the context of Google applications. This gives a lot of cloud computing power to you.
https://developers.google.com/apps-script/overview

1. If I produce a weekly report that interprets and advises the business, I should run the report daily. The average of 7 days of business operations is likely similar to 6 days. The results and conclusions of a report produced on Thursday will likely be the same as those produced on Friday.

2. If the Friday run fails, I have my conclusions from Thursday. If my Thursday run fails, I have early notice that the Friday run is likely to fail.

By working at one unit finer of granularity, you have given yourself lead time on potential issues and created a fall-back plan in case of catastrophic failure.

In the past, this has resulted in

1. ~3000 employees (myself included) getting paid for 13 days instead of not getting paid at all

2. A JIT system (a life-safety service) being able to estimate demand early so that key staff could attend a funeral.

3. Countless times, I did not have to do overtime because a combination of poor null handling and weird data caused fails, but (thankfully) days in advance.

These are the same principles from my High school Math and Physics classes: use one decimal place more to calculate than you report. In business reporting, if you are tracking dollars, calculate in cents; if you are tracking cents, do your calculations in <u>fractions of a penny</u>[40].

---

[40] Microsoft has a datatype known as "money". This object is an integer value but maintains 4 decimal places. I have used this to good effect to determine that my maths are absolutely correct to the penny when questioned.

Push and Pull

Push notifications change the playing field. Rather than updating the data on a schedule, we advertise changes to interested parties. However, we are *still constrained to the response time of our slowest observer.* Even in the case of nuclear blast detection, the point was to log and collect the data for interpretation by humans at a later date.

Take my trading bot: It sends me text notifications almost immediately (magnitude of seconds). This is faster and far more convenient/reliable than me checking once a day. However, it does not mean I can respond any faster. Real-time is constrained by the speed at which I **receive the information** and the speed at which I **can respond.** If I am trapped in a meeting, a secure network environment, or up to my waist in a river while fishing, I may not be able to initiate the trade for a couple of hours.

Lazy Loading Improves Net Performance

So if, in most (human) cases, it is sufficient to deal with timescales of minutes or hours, then we can conclude that the reports do not need to be updated any faster.

In general, updates do not need to be generated more frequently than they will be consumed by the observer (either digital, human, or system). This idea is where push notifications can both help and hurt us.

Polling (regular pulls) of source systems generates needless processing effort. Requesting information comes

---

https://learn.microsoft.com/en-us/office/vba/language/reference/user-interface-help/currency-data-type at a processing cost, and both systems need to expend effort talking to one another. If the system does not change, all of that effort results in no change.

Push notifications allow us to reduce this overhead by having the source system transmit change notifications to interested parties if something changes. This means that processing is performed when something needs updating.

However, given our sub-hour threshold for real-time, we may receive notice of change more frequently than we need to report it, and we may end up recalculating a report more frequently than it can be observed.

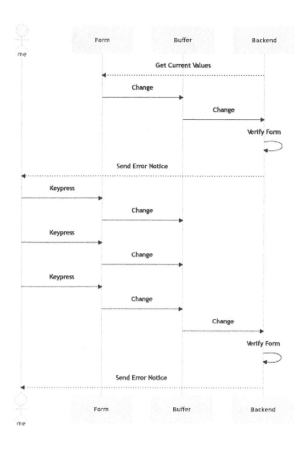

This was most evident in a simple web app I recently worked on. I wanted the user to receive real-time notification of the correctness of their entry into the form.

Every change to the form results in a change event processed by the back end. I followed the error notifications from the validation and tried to type in a valid value to observe the update coming back to the form.

I was being driven crazy. I was only 10 characters away from a positive result, but I kept getting stopped by each keypress as it recalculated the validity. Each key press pushed a notification to the back end, triggering a recalculation ... but I could already see I was wrong. Internally, I was begging the system to just let me finish typing.

In the end, I put a timer on the validation: do not update it more frequently than every 23 milliseconds. That little bit of delay allowed me to finish typing, and the quality of the feedback did not suffer (maybe even improved) by bringing it to the human scale.

 Buffering results until someone wants them takes us back to <u>lazy loading</u>. If nobody will read your data, don't bother calculating it. This reduces overhead because you may have 20 updates but only one view (and, therefore, calculation).

If you are speaking about push notifications, you should think about lazy loading. A push notification can be used to notify our system that it needs to update, but we can use Lazy Loading to defer that processing until it is needed. But it is a balancing act. We can defer processing, but we also need to balance it with performing it frequently enough.

Conclusion

Most of us are not attempting to detect the oncoming wave of a nuclear blast, nor are we racing ahead of a Solar Flare about to destroy the multi-billion dollar data on our international network infrastructure. Most of us operate on a timescale of minutes or hours, well within the operating tolerances of even the most basic of desktop computers.

Given this, we need to remember two key points

1. Time scales dictate real-time

2. You should always be processing one unit of time smaller than will be consumed

We can scale our response time to an *appropriate* level through lazy-loading and push notifications. An aircraft trying to stay airborne requires a scale different from inventory management in a retail organization.

Inundating humans with data does not improve information uptake.

Having said that, we want to keep ahead of our audience. We can deliver information faster and more frequently than people need it, there is therefore no reason to have it standing by ready for them when they want it. There is no reason for us to not do our checks and balances well in advance.

The key is balance.

Don't let sales tactics (and your own ego and machoism) make you forget that every solution has its own set of drawbacks and is subject to the law of diminishing returns.

At some point, we need to recognize that the problem is solved and the solution is good enough.

Once real-time moves past observable, getting faster is wasted time.

146

Really Simple, Simple Messaging Service

Sending Text Alerts for Dummy Programmers

- Simple Messaging Solution: Learn how to set up SMS notifications using email-to-SMS services from North American cellular providers.

- Cost-Effective Approach: Discover a budget-friendly method for automating alerts without the need for expensive third-party services.

- Practical Implementation: Follow step-by-step instructions and code examples to create your own SMS notification system using Google Apps Script integrated with Google Sheets.

 Sample Code Available

Before I began my journey in the field of Software and Data, I started a career in Nursing.

I spent many days working in a hospital with the ward's pager stuck to my belt. The point of this pager was that if there was an emergency, all staff could be recalled to their ward to assist with the emergency. Even though most people owned a cell phone, pagers were passive radio devices that were safe to carry around sensitive equipment.

Fast-forward a couple of years to my first job as a Software Developer. Working for a small consulting company, it was only a short time before I was pressed into the on-call rotation and handed the on-call cell phone. The point was that when something terrible happened, the customer representative would call you to fix problems that customers experienced. Often, remote login and restart a crashed service.

It occurred to me (kind of obviously) that we could automate the system checks and, just as I experienced in the hospital, send a notification out to pagers, potentially resolving issues even before the customer noticed a problem. (I know, revolutionary thinking)

There were two arguments against this idea:

1. We would not catch all the problems

2. It was really expensive.

It took everything I had to keep calm about the first point, but my glare communicated my opinion of it effectively.

The second point was very valid.

Phones capable of receiving email without a WiFi router were a long way away (or prohibitively expensive). Pagers were cheap enough, but implementing an automated pager service via the APIs was wildly pricey. I don't remember the exact cost, but I remember looking at the amount, comparing it to my pay cheque, and deciding I would rather myself and my co-workers get paid.

It was one of those problems that always irked me enough that I thought about it but not enough for me to chase it down.

About 10 years later, I was on contract with a major university, working on their communications platform. We were running some tests on the website's emergency banner, and I joked that we should implement an SMS service for students.

With a twinkle in his eye, the lead developer said they already had and let me in on one of the industry's greatest secrets: a free SMS service is already built into all North American cellular provider services.

I am going to show you how to create your own SMS notification system.

While I have used this technique several times over the years, the only implementation I still have access to is Google Application Script (GAS)[41]. GAS is a JavaScript implementation used to enhance documents in the Google Office Suite. One of the advantages of using an online Spreadsheet was that it had scheduled tasks, and the computer was always on. Effectively, it is a cheap computing engine. All samples will assume GAS.

---

[41] Google Apps Script
https://developers.google.com/apps-script/

The Trick

The really simple trick is that service providers in North America all provide an email to SMS service. Every phone number in North America has a corresponding email address.

The service providers do not widely advertise it, but it is not hidden either. All that needs to be done is to send a carefully crafted email to the phone number's email address. The email address domain will depend on the provider:

Bell Mobility	txt.bell.ca
Fido	fido.ca
MTS	text.mtsmobility.com
Sasktel	sms.sasktel.com
Telus	msg.telus.com
Virgin	vmobile.ca

Given this information, the phone number `(403)123-4567`, and knowing that the carrier is Shaw, email to `4031234567@txt.shawmobile.ca`.

Different providers satisfy this in different ways, and when I have changed providers, I have found receiving messages without jumping through some hoops difficult. To confirm it is working on your phone, send yourself a text message from your email.

Sending Notifications

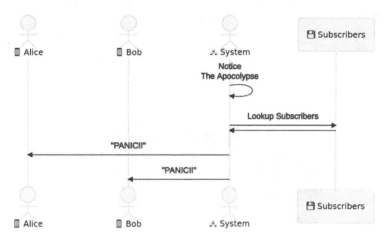

The alert system is fairly straightforward

The system is pretty straightforward. It is designed to identify the occurrence of an event and notify a list of people. Traditionally, sending an alert email to administrators has been a common and fundamental requirement. Mail Merges are an even more venerable process.

Our system will go through three phases:

1. Identify that a notification must be sent

2. Identify who to send the notification to

3. Send the notification

Many details need to be handled to do this correctly, but for the most part, these are the three phases of our system.

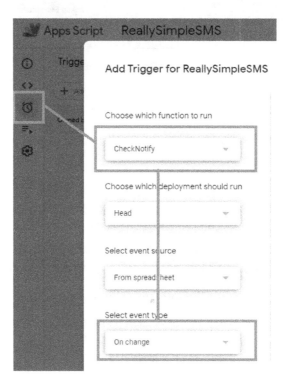

Your system would naturally decide to notify: it could be a system failure, a patient calling for help, or an inbound solar flare. For demonstration purposes, we are using a change in the status of a cell block in a spreadsheet that will be polled every 15 minutes.

Once we have identified that a notification should be sent, we need to find the appropriate people to whom it should be sent.

```
const book = SpreadsheetApp.getActiveSpreadsheet();

function CheckNotify(){
  let config = book.getSheetByName('Config');
  let notify = config.getRange(1,2);
  if(notify[0][0]){
    notify.setRange([[false]]);
    Notify();
  }
}

function Notify() {
  let subs = book.getSheetByName('Subscribers');
  let emails = subs

.getRange(2,2,subscribers.getLastRow(),2).getValues()
    .map((d)=>{ return `${d[0]}@${d[1]}`; })
    .filter(d=>{return d !== '@';})
    .join(',')
    ;
  MailApp.sendEmail({
    to: 'example@example.com', bcc: emails,
    subject: 'PANIC!!',
    body: 'Please, take appropriate action.'
  });
}
```

To identify them, we simply look up a list of emails from the subscriber table and loop through it.

The email will be sent **from** the spreadsheet owner. Notice the use of **BCC**, which is a good practice to balance the number of emails sent and protect the privacy interests of the subscribers. Alternatively, send an email to each subscriber individually.

It is often helpful to send to both text and email where the email version has a table of actions that must be taken (using the **htmlBody** instead of **body**). This lets you receive a quick notice that you have to get to a computer and get more details once you are there.

Untrusted Subscribers

This tiny process is fine for a team looking for notifications of a failed system, the build has been completed, or the automated tests failed. In fact, adding your phone number and figuring out who your provider is sounds like an excellent initiation task as part of onboarding new members

... actually, that's a really good idea. I may have to update the onboarding documentation at work.

On a small team, everyone is trusted and responsible for adding themselves. The list is small enough to manage by hand. To some extent, you don't have to worry about people maliciously adding their ex's phone number or later claiming they did not request the subscription.

As systems get bigger, they get more complex.

Let us change the purpose of the system. Let us assume we are detecting a Zombie Apocalypse. The wider public may be interested in hearing about it. In this scenario, we could add a web form that allows people to subscribe to our Zombie Apocalypse Alert system. Of course, not everybody believes in zombies, so we need to confirm that subscriptions are from people who want them.

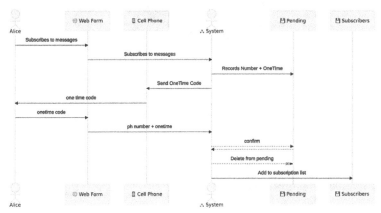

A registration process is possible that verifies ownership of the phone.

The most straightforward mechanism for verification is just to ask the person, and it has been the most common means since email notifications were a thing. We can ask them for their phone number (perhaps through a web form), associate that phone number with a secret, and then send the secret to that phone number. If they give us the secret, they indicate that we won't be annoying them by sending messages in the future.

This exact mechanism works for mailing addresses, email addresses, or any other form of location authentication (like OAuth)

```
function CheckForNewNumbers(){
  let submits = book.getSheetByName('Submitted');
  let verifies =
submits.getRange(2,1,submits.getLastRow(),3);
  let values = verifies.getValues();
  for(let verify of values){
```

```javascript
    if(verify[0] === '') continue;
    HandleNewNumber(...verify);
    verify.fill('');
  }
  verifies.setValues(values);
}


function HandleNewNumber(name,phone,provider){
  // generate a verification token
  let onetime = Math.round(Math.random()*9999);
  // make it 4-digits
  onetime = `0000${onetime}`
    .split('').reverse().slice(0,4).join('');
  // set a one hour timeout
  let timeout = new Date();
  timeout.setHours(timeout.getHours()+1);
  // send the token to the person
  MailApp.sendEmail({
    to: `${phone}@${provider}`,
    subject: 'Code ' + onetime,
    body: 'Your onetime code is ' + onetime
  });
  // save the values to the pending table
  let pendings = book.getSheetByName('Pending');
  let row = pendings.getRange(pendings.getLastRow()+1,1,1,5);
  row.setValues([[name,phone,provider,onetime,timeout]]);
}
```

The **onetime** token is a randomly generated number that is large enough to be somewhat distinct and small enough that it is convenient for a human to enter. A **timeout** of one hour ensures it fails if no one actions it immediately; an exploiter cannot use a forgotten code. Once we store the token and share it with the target device, we have a means of knowing we are communicating with the intended audience.

Once the subscriber comes to us with their identifying number (their phone number) and the token we shared with them, we have a way for them to demonstrate they want to continue.

```
function VerifyToken(phone,token){
  // grab a time stamp that we are going to use
  let now = new Date();
  // find the "pending" table
  let pendings = book.getSheetByName('Pending');
  pendings =
pendings.getRange(2,1,pendings.getLastRow(),5);
  let rows = pendings.getValues();
  for(let row of rows){
    // if the row has expired
    if (now > row[4]) {
      // delete the row's contents
      row.fill('');
      // and ignore it
      continue;
    }
    // if phone number and token match the row
    if (row[1] === phone && row[3] === token){
      // put it in the subscriber's table
      let subs = book.getSheetByName('Subscribers');
      subs = subs.getRange(subs.getLastRow()+1,1,1,3);
      subs.setValues([row.slice(0,3)]);
      row.fill('');
    }
  }
  pendings.setValues(rows);
}
```

It is important to remember this demonstration example has been simplified for understanding. Several things can be adjusted to improve security:

- the `random` function could use a strong cryptographic version

- the size of the token could be increased, making it harder to guess

- the timeout could be shortened, decreasing the number of guesses that can be attempted

Further improvements are possible, such as removing expired token rows (to prevent the database from growing too much), controlling the number of instances of a single phone number that are stored (to prevent a DDOS attack), placing a time limit between attempts to validate (reducing the number of guesses possible). Also, I like using `Date.now()` rather than `new Date()` because dealing with an `int` is more accessible for me to wrap my head around when it comes time to step through the code.

Detecting the Provider

If you are reading this article, it is likely because you did not know about this service. It's, therefore, reasonable to expect our general public subscribers to not know about it either. Asking them to remember their exact provider and distinguish it from similar names (`vmobl` or `virginmobile`) and finding it in a drop-down are inconvenient.

It would be a vast improvement if we looked up their provider automatically, and given a list of carriers, we can.

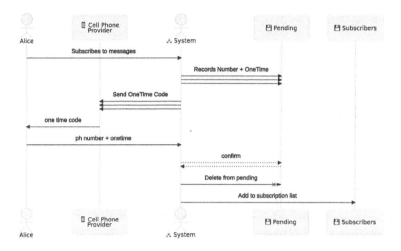

Our new process simply generates a unique one-time code **for each provider**. By attempting delivery to every provider and then waiting to see which one of the tokens got through, we can determine which provider the subscriber is using.

```
function CheckForNewNumbers(){
  let submits = book.getSheetByName('Submitted');
  submits = submits.getRange(2,1,submits.getLastRow(),3);
  let values = submits.getValues();
  let providers = book.getSheetByName('Providers');
  providers = providers
    .getRange(2,2,submits.getLastRow(),1)
    .getValues();
  for(let verify of values){
    if(verify[0] === '') continue;
    for(let provider of providers){
      verify[2] = provider[0];
      HandleSubmit(...verify);
    }
    verify.fill('');
```

```
    }
    submits.setValues(values);
}
```

Conclusion

I am unsure if this email-to-text capability is dictated by law or is just a custom that evolved over time, but it is certainly there for people to take advantage of. Rather than sending signals to a costly service, it is possible to send signals to cell phones cheaply.

One of the key advantages is that the infrastructure to build this is already available: email is ubiquitous. While the example was demonstrated in Google Application Script, I have implemented this solution in Java, Python, SAS, Powershell, and Bash. It is only limited by how your system sends emails.

Recently, I helped a team implement this to notify if one of their desktops was turned off. They are using their desktops as a linked network for distributed computing. Everyone working from home needed a way to be notified if a computer in the network got turned off. Each computer in the network will now send a notice if one of its peers is turned off.

If you are building a mission-critical system, I recommend using a consistent and well-supported API. Various providers offer various interpretations of the emails, leading to some "interesting" messages being received. A well-supported service mitigates this issue.

However, if you are a small team, just trying to get a prototype in place, frustrated with bureaucracy getting in the way, or just like to tinker, hopefully, this will get you started.

Standard Disaster Scenarios Your Business Needs to Prepare For

Planning for things to go wrong, for Dummy Programmers

- Critical Scenarios: Delve into four overlooked disaster scenarios crucial for system preparedness, offering insights for even the most confident programmers.

- Realistic Challenges: Explore scenarios like "Under the Bus" and "Bump on the Head," shedding light on potential disruptions beyond typical considerations.

- Practical Solutions: Gain valuable strategies and objection-handling techniques to fortify systems against unforeseen events and ensure resilience in adversity.

In any system design, there are several scenarios that should be considered to prevent system failure. Each of these scenarios describes a worst-case scenario that frames planning for catastrophic events.

Often, when describing the need for various emergency protocols, the presenter faces resistance, but we trust each other. These strawman arguments distract from the genuine underlying risk that needs to be addressed.

These descriptions and titles are meant to give a standardized response to the most common objections. Each scenario has a list of ways it presents in the real world. The titles are humorous to ease the tension, but the scenarios are serious and realistic.

The scenarios are also meant to be non-specific. Rather than planning for specific events, general scenarios encompassing general responses allow for adaptation to multiple considerations.

1. Under the Bus

2. Bump on the Head

3. Spiked Drink

4. Sword of God

5. Daemonic Possession

Under the Bus

The primary on a system got run over by a bus on the way to work and has been hospitalized for an indeterminate amount of time.

Presentation

Any unavailability of the system experts, potentially combined with the need for action

- Accident: sky-diving, home repair, car accident

- Vacation: phoning people while they are on vacation is rude

- Illness: myocarditis, kidney stones, haemorrhoids, common cold

- Arrest: sometimes people get detained; rightly or wrongly

Objections

That's a horrible thing to say

If it makes you feel better, they are going to be OK, but accidents happen in life. Do you really want to be the person who is phoning a colleague while they should be resting in the hospital?

We had better make sure staff didn't do anything risky.

Go review that with your HR department. Informing employees that they are not permitted to have hobbies outside work is dangerous.

Bump on the Head

One of the trusted individuals has recently received a bump on the head and now has a brain injury that has drastically altered their personality. They can no longer be trusted. It is unclear how long they were trusted when they should not have been.

Presentation

- Blackmail: or possibly bribery, where an outside actor has altered the state of the trust relationship

- Poor trust evaluation: You shouldn't have trusted them in the first place[42]

- External system breach: a trusted individual has had their digital identity compromised.

- An actual bump on the head has caused people's personalities to dramatically change[43]

Objections

It's OK, I trust you.

This statement exposes employees to risk, placing an unfair responsibility on them.

---

[42] Why psychopaths are so good at getting ahead
https://www.cnbc.com/2016/11/18/why-psychopaths-are
-so-good-at-getting-ahead.html
[43] Phineas Gage is the most famous "Bump on the Head" in history
https://en.wikipedia.org/wiki/Phineas_Gage

The minute something goes wrong, employees should have evidence that they were acting within acceptable parameters and that the managerial staff had accepted any risks associated with the action. If judgment calls were required, and bad things happened, employees need to have a clear line of approval in place that they can point to as having failed (justifying their taking action)

Spiked Drink

The trusted individual stands up from lunch and realizes they are feeling wobbly. Someone spiked their drink.

Presentation

Any scenario where the actor has a compromised capacity for judgement

- Woken in the middle of the night

- Family emergencies

- Had a couple of drinks, heavy pain medication

- Compromised judgement results in the inability to judge yourself compromised.

- Snap decisions

Plan for individuals to be able to declare themselves incapacitated or compromised; plan for them to take action even when their judgement is compromised; plan to declare someone else's judgement as compromised. Have clear instructions to reduce the need for judgment; the time to make a plan is before the emergency.

Objections

People aren't allowed to drink on duty.

Being on-call, or worse, being the second or third person on call, during an emergency can activate you at unanticipated times. The only way to avoid this is to consider all staff on-call 24/365, which is clearly unreasonable.

Sword of God

(aka Sodom and Gomorrah, Meteor Impact, Zombies)

A meteor has just hit the facility. Where there was a service centre, there is now a crater.

If it makes you feel better, everyone in the region is OK but more than a little distracted.

Presentation

Any regional outage that results in an entire service being lost. Limited to no staff in the region able to respond.

- Power outage

- Natural Disaster (storm, tsunami, earthquake)

- Epidemic

- War

- Civil Disruption (protest, riot)

Objections

Don't be over-dramatic

During the 2005 Ice Storm in Montreal, a colleague's phone rang with a request for technical assistance from another company. The company, located in Montreal, had been without power for two days. Generators had been activated, and the facility was operational; however, due to the high demand for fuel replenishment and the state of infrastructure, they could not secure more diesel. Their three-day supply was about to run out.

A heroic effort was undertaken; unfortunately, due to the massive infrastructure disruption, we could not rebuild their services on our infrastructure before the fuel ran out ... leaving hundreds of thousands of Canadians without service for weeks.

Dæmonic Possession

(aka Planetary Alignment, Plumb Bad Luck)

You've done everything perfectly, but a small dæmon is inside your computer. As you type your solution, it waits inside for an inopportune moment and messes something up. Something important.

Presentation

Software systems are complex, and complex systems are just that ... complex. Complexity leads to unpredictability, and that is basically random behaviour. This can present in all kinds of ways, none of them predictable.

- fat-fingering, typos

- stuff just stops working ... nobody knows why

Objections

If I can't predict it, how can I plan for it

This is fatalism, giving up, and that we must not do.

 Preparing for bizarro land is not easy, but it is possible. Generally, this is done through constant testing and rehearsal (you are rehearsing disasters, aren't you). This forces people to practice system failures and general recovery under controlled circumstances.

Conclusion

Published initially on my private consultancy website in 2013, this became something I wanted to preserve, share, and keep living. I have shared it with every company I have worked with, but it needs to be more widely distributed because I have yet to see a company that can handle all of these scenarios.

De-duplicating Data Storage in Data Science

How to Not Store the Same File Twice

- Introduction to Data De-duplication: explores the concept of de-duplicating data storage

- Addressing Duplicate File Storage: discusses the prevalence of duplicate files in large file share systems.

- Optimizing Storage Costs: presents de-duplication as a solution to reduce physical storage requirements by showcasing potential cost savings and efficiency gains.

Many years ago, I read an article about Google's internal labs creating a sha1 hash collision between two PDF documents[44]. The documents were very different, but through clever bit manipulation, they resulted in identical sha1 codes. It was a fascinating read for a Friday afternoon, but over the weekend, I started to ask the question: Why does Google care?

One significant place where this would impact Google would be on their storage platform, Google Drive. Given that they are storing massive numbers of files on behalf of massive numbers of people, there will, in all probability, be a massive number of duplicate files.

Logically, this is likely true through its usage. Assume I engage in a real estate transaction, exchanging emailed PDFs with scanned signatures is not uncommon. Assuming everyone is using Google Drive to back up their documents, four people have copies of the same document: the buyer, the buyer's agent, the seller's agent, and the seller. Remember to add lawyers and lenders later in the process.

I have worked for organizations whose primary business involved the interchange and storage of data (Oil/Gas Production, Telecommunications, or Data Repositories). In every case, our solution to the problem was simple: charge the customer. Charge the customer the variable cost as a rate per byte. Multiply the

- amount of drive space they take up

---

[44] SHAttered, gives a summary of the findings and links to the relevant researchers.
https://shattered.io/

174

- replications space

- server cost

- electricity

- rent

- markup

Charging the customer is an excellent way to offset the cost, and Google does bill its customers. However, it is possible to maintain the same revenue through de-duplication while drastically reducing the amount of physical storage.

Take the GSMA-RCC[45] specification, which states that images can be interchanged between client devices and should be retained on the server for later pickup. So, if a meme goes viral, thousands of individuals may forward the image to one another, resulting in thousands of copies of that image flying across the network and being stored on server drives.

Further, if it's a good meme, people will forward it back to people they know who have already received it. The image goes round and round, and it only stops once it has theoretically been sent on every possible communication between pairs of people..

---

[45] Rich Communication Suite - Advanced Communications, Services and Client Specification, Version 11.0
https://www.gsma.com/futurenetworks/wp-content/uploads/2019/10/RCC.07-v11.0.pdf

With 10 billion devices on the planet[46], more than Seven Bridges need to be crossed.

If some jerk sends that meme as a bitmap, each image instance takes up about 1079KB.

• $1.00 per MB revenue • $0.90 per MB cost • 1,000,000 user interactions (transfer) • 1024KB file	= datasize * transfers * (revenue - cost) = 1 MB * 1million * ($1 - $0.9) = 1TB of storage = **$100,000 profit**

We can be sensible about it and require that everything is converted to PNG (notice Google asks to do this for Google Photos), reducing the size to 615KB (60%). This is useful when dealing with a fixed revenue where people are paying a flat fee, but lossy compression is not a true copy of data and is not feasible for legal and science datasets.

---

[46] Digital Devices Are the Backbone of Every Organisation –Are You Managing Them Properly
https://technative.io/digital-devices-are-the-backbone-of-every-organisation-are-you-managing-them-properly/

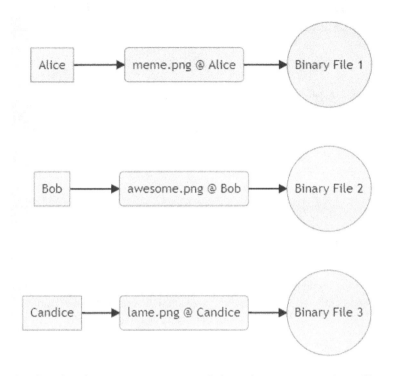

Storing the object once per person is how the users perceive a file system

Storing the image once per person receiving it is an inefficient use of resources. If, on the other hand, we can identify that it is the same image, we can reduce our cost to **storing only one instance but charging for each transfer**.

<ul><li>$1.00 per MB revenue</li><li>$0.90 per MB cost</li><li>1,000,000 user interactions (transfer)</li><li>1024KB file</li></ul>	= (datasize * transfers * revenue) - (datasize * cost) = (1MB * 1million * $1) - (1MB * $0.9) = 1MB of storage **= $999,999.10 profit**

There is a big difference between having a cost of 90¢ per transaction and a cost of 90¢.

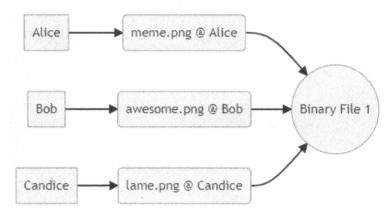

Identifying that everyone is storing the same data, allows us to significantly reduce the amount of space we consume while giving the same level of service to our users.

However, de–duplication is not an easy problem to solve.

First, we receive the files independently of one another from different people with different names. Since we have many large files, comparing them byte–by–byte will take significant processing power to every other stored file. In a large–scale system, this simply is not feasible.

This brings us back to where we began: Google had managed to cause a collision between sha1 in the lab. Why would they have been concerned with researching the extreme possibilities of collision in binary documents? Because they use hash to help identify the uniqueness of files.

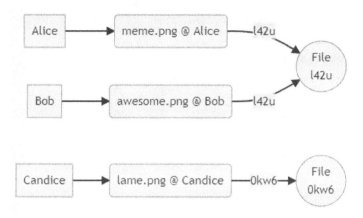

We can use large hashes as primary keys for the files.

A Working Example

Pulling on some experience solving this problem using CouchDB, we can implement an in-browser demonstration of the principles involved using JavaScript and PouchDB. If you are not familiar with PouchDB and using its DB interface, read the definitive introduction by Nolan Lawson[47].

We will create a simple example with three users (Alice, Bob, and Carol) sharing their favourite lines from a new Opera[48] they just saw.

---

[47] Secondary indexes have landed in PouchDB, 2014-05-01
https://pouchdb.com/2014/05/01/secondary-indexes-have-landed-in-pouchdb.html
[48] The Pirate Movie, 1987. Not quite The Pirates of Penzance, but close enough.
https://www.youtube.com/watch?v=i1gt1yvUC-s&t=1850s

```
let db = new PouchDB('filestore');
async function main(){
  await db.destroy();
  db = new PouchDB('filestore');
  await CreateIndex();
await save(
    'alice',
    'gilbert.txt',
    'I am the very model of a modern major general'
  );
  await save(
    'bob',
    'sullivan.txt',
    'I am the very model of a modern major general'
  );
  await save(
    'carol',
    'gilbert.txt',
    'I have knowledge of things animal, vegetable and
mineral'
  );
  await save(
    'alice',
    'sullivan.txt',
    'I have knowledge of things animal, vegetable and
mineral'
  );
  let data = await db.allDocs({include_docs:true});
  console.log(`DB Size: ${JSON.stringify(data).length}`);

  console.log(await dload('alice'  ,'gilbert.txt'));
  console.log(await dload('bob'    ,'sullivan.txt'));
  console.log(await dload('carol','gilbert.txt'));
  let peruser = await db.query('allfiles',{
    reduce:true,
    group:true,
    group_level: 1
```

```
  });
  console.log(peruser);
}
main();
```

The process is relatively straightforward: three people store one of two lines of text in their account and then retrieve them from the database.

Of interest is the total size being stored, as well as the per-user size (billable size) usage:

```
DB Size: 1813 bytes

| User  | Files | Size |
| :---- | ----: | ---: |
| alice |     2 |  101 |
| bob   |     1 |   45 |
| carol |     1 |   56 |
```

The real meat of the program is in the save and dload functions, which abstract away the interactions with the database. Further, CreateIndex defines the mechanism for search and retrieval.

```
async function CreateIndex(){
  return await db.put({
    _id: '_design/allfiles',
    views: {
      'allfiles': {
        map: function (doc) {
```

```
            var userpath = [doc.user,doc.path];
            emit(userpath,doc.size);
          }.toString(),
          reduce:'_stats'
      }
    }
  });
}

async function save(user,filename,blob){
  return db.put({
    _id: [user,filename].join('@'),
    user:user,
    path:filename,
    size:blob.length,
    _attachments: {
      '0': {
        content_type: 'text/plain',
        data: window.btoa(blob)
      }
    }
  });
}

async function dload(user,filename){
  let recs = await db.query('allfiles',{
    reduce: false,
    include_docs: true,
    attachments: true,
    key: [user,filename]
  });
  let blob = recs.rows[0].doc._attachments['0'].data;
  blob = window.atob(blob);
  return blob;
}
```

The save and download functions work on the assumption that we are going to store a copy of the record for each person, while the index manages a list of users and their files.

User	File	Size	Min	Avg	Max
alice	2	101	45	50	56
bob	1	45	45	45	45
carol	1	56	56	56	56

```
DB Size..: 1814 bytes
Billable.:  202 bytes
```

 De-duplcation I - Before
JSFiddle giving an example of the working demonstration

Reducing Storage

To modify this example to reduce our storage, we must first change the **save** function to not blindly save for each user but instead save each **BLOB** as a primary object and track users observing it as a secondary item.

```
async function save(user, filename, blob) {
  let hash = new TextEncoder().encode(blob);
  hash = await crypto.subtle.digest('SHA-256', hash);
  hash = Array.from(new Uint8Array(hash));
  hash = hash
    .map(b => b.toString(16).padStart(2, '0'))
    .join('')
```

```
    .substr(0,4);
let userpath = [user, filename].join('@');
let rec = null;
try {
  rec = await db.get(hash);
}
catch (e) {
  if (e.status !== 404) throw e;
  // create the object, with a list of user's using it
  rec = {
    _id: hash,
    userpaths: [],
    size: blob.length,
    _attachments: {
      '0': {
        content_type: 'text/plain',
        data: window.btoa(blob)
      }
    }
  }
}
if (!rec.userpaths.includes(userpath)) {
  rec.userpaths.push(userpath);
}
// finally save the record
return db.put(rec);
}
```

This ensures that we only ever store a blob once.

Using the hash as the record identifier means that no
matter how many times it is submitted, we just keep using
the existing record. New users are simply added to the list
of users using the item. Users can even make copies of it by
submitting the same item with a different name; we keep

184

adding notes that the user has their own name for that
record.

Naturally, this breaks the lookup index we were using. The
original index used the record name (username+path) to
look up the file, but the file no longer uses this as its record
name. Instead, we need to create a lookup index
constructed from all the users who use the same file.

```
async function CreateIndex() {
   await db.put({
      _id: '_design/allfiles',
      views: {
         'allfiles': {
            map: function(doc) {
               for (let userpath of doc.userpaths) {
                  userpath = userpath.split('@');
                  emit(userpath, doc.size);
               }
            }.toString(),
            reduce: '_stats'
         }
      }
   });
}
```

By looping through each user's paths, we have updated our
index to return the underlying file for each *file use*. This
means no change to our download function, as the view's
interface has not changed.

Note that we included the file size in the view and used the
`stats` reduce method. This means that when it comes time
to bill, we can simply add up the number of blobs the user
references and their total size.

Re-running `main` gives us a new total size and billing data:

```
DB Size: 1109 bytes

| User  | Files | Size |
| :---- | ----: | ---: |
| alice |     2 |  101 |
| bob   |     1 |   45 |
| carol |     1 |   56 |
```

Even in our trivial example, with a very small content size,
our database size (and therefore our business expenses)
decreased by a whopping 39%. A better return is seen as
the ratio of storage size shifts toward content and less
with metadata (think MP3, MP4, and PNG).

Also, notice that the billable sizes stayed the same.

User	File	Size	Min	Avg	Max
alice	2	101	45	50	56
bob	1	45	45	45	45
carol	1	56	56	56	56

```
DB Size..: 1109 bytes
Billable.:  202 bytes
```

De-duplcation I - After
same example as previously presented but with the
changes to make the storage smaller.

Completing the Solution

After all of that, we cannot forget that Google demonstrated that collisions are maliciously possible, therefore they cannot be absolutely trusted. We must perform complete byte-by-byte comparisons. **Hash functions are useful tools for determining dissimilarity between binary objects, not for determining similarity.**[49]

This is a handy feature. We can quickly narrow the required comparisons to almost nothing using a large hash. There is a good chance I will have no more than one match that needs to be checked, which is significantly less effort than millions. Once I've narrowed it down, the complete file must be checked with an extra marker to distinguish it from the one we already have.

A second problem is that we need to delete records at some point. In this case, we can simply drop the user's reference to the object, though we must also observe for the time when no user has a reference to the object. When all references to the object are removed, the object itself should be removed. Similarly, if a record is renamed, we must remove the old reference before creating the new one.

I leave these as exercises for the reader.

Further Reading

This demonstration uses JavaScript and PouchDB. I love in-browser protests because they are so portable: you

---

[49] See the chapter "Using WebGL to Solve a Practical Problem" for a solution to probabilistic matching of similar large objects.

always have a debugger and runtime environment available.

PouchDB is a JavaScript implementation of CouchDB. One of the large-scale CouchDB implementations would be a good start to expand the solution to something useful at the enterprise level.

It is also worth mentioning that this technique is not limited to any particular system. The same method could be implemented at the Operating System level using symbolic or hard links[50]. In fact, some database and FS storage combinations may be an optimized approach.

 Manual: Apache CouchDB

 Manual: CouchBase

 Manual: IBM CloudAnt

 Creating indexes: Secondary Indexes have landed in PouchDB

---

[50]

https://www.howtogeek.com/287014/how-to-create-and -use-symbolic-links-aka-symlinks-on-linux/

[How to Create and Use Symbolic Links (aka Symlinks) on Linux](#)

 [What is ZFS?](#) A file system that has de-duplication built-in

190

Not storing (almost) the same file twice

De-duplicating Data Storage using Delta Files

- De-duplicating Data Storage: Addressing the challenge of redundant data storage and the impact on storage costs.

- Data Revisions and Storage Overhead: Accumulating historic datasets over time, leading to significant storage costs.

- Cost-Effective Solutions: Introducing techniques to reduce storage costs through automated data management strategies.

GitLab code sample that generates a sample historic change set off data.

A notebook demonstrating the cost savings you can achieve.

In the previous chapter, I showed a technique for reducing the storage load on a system that encounters multiple copies of the same file. This is a fairly common situation in data-intensive environments, as data scientists make copies of the dataset they are working on, their colleagues are working on, and they share it with their friends. Applying the techniques, we showed a 36% profit increase in a laboratory scenario.

Another widespread behaviour is **Data Revisions**.

Naturally, our source datasets change over time, changing our output datasets. While most people think of keeping all data forever, for the most part, we are only concerned with the current state. However, FOMO keeps us from removing now historic but redundant datasets. Over time, this data continuously grows,

I'm going to share a way to reduce this cost by 90% over 3 years.

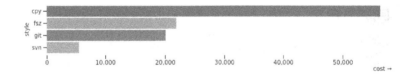

90% savings in 3rd year

An example from my past was a heat map of financial transactions across Canada. This dataset was based on the last two years of economic data aggregated at the Postal Code level. To place the items on the map, we had a second dataset of financial districts and a third set of postal codes and their corresponding financial district. To add a layer of complexity, Canada Post changes its postal delivery routes regularly and, therefore, its postal codes, as the boundaries of our financial districts change periodically. This means that the proportion of a Postal Code that resides within the Financial District[51] needs to be more consistent and requires constant updating from a third-party provider[52].

The network drive folder looked something like this:

```
name                        size
------------------------------------------
/proj/1/dashboard.html      12 KB
/proj/1/transactions.tns    50  B
/proj/1/postalcodes.csv     33 MB [ref]
/proj/1/districts.gml       37 MB [ref]
------------------------------------------
                            70 MB
```

So, we have three datasets:

- Our live financial data (a live connection)

- A listing of postal codes

- A listing of location shapes

---

[51] World Map Subdivisions, All first-level subdivisions (provinces, states, counties, etc.) for every country in the world.
https://www.mapchart.net/world-subdivisions.html
[52] Nominatim, Open-source geocoding with OpenStreetMap data
https://nominatim.org/

The relationship between the datasets and the final aggregate that is displayed on the dashboard can be described as

```
select
  d.label,
  d.shape,
  sum(p.weight * t.amt) as amt
from
  transactions t
  inner join postal p on f.postal_code = p.code
  inner join districts d on d.id = p.district_id
```

While the financial summary is updated in real-time, we receive updated districts and postal codes every quarter. A reasonably regular practice is that we receive an email with a link to a CSV file every quarter, and someone has to download the file and overwrite the current CSV files. However, it is considered a best practice to make a copy of the old files in an archive folder. This is done by creating a copy and date-stamping it.

```
name                           size
-----------------------------------------
/proj/1/
  dashboard.html               12 KB
  districts.gml                37 MB
  postalcodes.csv              33 MB
  arch/
    districts.202203.csv       37 MB
    districts.202204.csv       37 MB
    postalcodes.202203.csv     33 MB
    postalcodes.202204.csv     33 MB
```

194

```
 ---------------------------------------------
                             Total: 210 MB
```

Many people recognize this pattern of file management as very common. It is also easy to see how this can spiral out of control.

- Notice that this is `proj/1` of ... let's say about 100 active projects.

- These projects have been running longer than 2 months (an average of 5 years)

- We have implemented a basic audit and recovery policy requiring redundant backups of the drive space, with point-in-time recovery capabilities (daily for a month, monthly for 10 years)

Given these approximations, we have quickly consumed 210MB (a tiny project) of data per project, with 60 months of user copies, on slow archival disks with 150 disk snapshots, and 100 projects. A total of 180 TB. The policies and project volumes are all realistic; I suspect I'm underestimating the storage demand. Assuming <u>AWS S3 Standard storage</u>[53] of the files (USD 0.021/GB), this costs $70,000/year (CAD).

---

[53] Amazon S3 Pricing, 2024-04-12
https://aws.amazon.com/s3/pricing/

It's not my money ... why should I care?

Two events made me care:

1. A colleague was denied access to the service because of concerns about disk consumption and cost, and their business case write-up did not persuade the executives. This was a significant loss to the organization.

2. A different colleague asked to recover a single file from a historic checkpoint. The backup team informed him they would need to find a disk big enough to restore the point in time. The backup team needed to restore the entirety of all the projects to get one file, a significant expense to the organization.

These are demonstrations of bureaucracy getting in the way. They stem from a poor understanding of digital storage and information management techniques by the IT department and the Data Scientists.

Sometimes, we must keep stuff moving, even when bureaucracy gets in the way.

A Quick History Lesson

The disk usage pattern in question is well-established and intuitive, usually developed by students in their first year of college. Changes made to complex systems can result in unanticipated outcomes. It is also not always obvious which change (or combination of changes) led to the behaviour; having old copies can help you understand what has gone wrong.

Having identified only the portions of a file that have changed, the fundamental problem becomes very recognizable to most programmers (actually most content publishers) as Change Management or Version Control. Over the decades, several tools have evolved to manage this problem, called <u>version control systems (VCS)</u>. While the field is littered with VCS, a few prominent ones represent significant changes in how changes are thought of and managed.

CVS	1985	Changes to individual files are tracked independently
SVN	2000	Related changes to multiple files are considered a single unit
Git	2005	Collections of changes can be managed as independent units

These three tools represent essential changes in understanding how the databases we store data revisions should be structured.

It is essential to see the differences between instances in a large volume of data. Asking what has changed in large volumes of data can take a lot of work. Difference tools (`diff`-ing) became standard in the data and programming toolkit (<u>`diff`</u>) in the mid-70s. Further, tools like <u>`patch`</u> offer a way to transmit (or store) only the changes, which may be significantly smaller than an entire copy. There are now a plethora of <u>graphical tools</u> for such tasks.

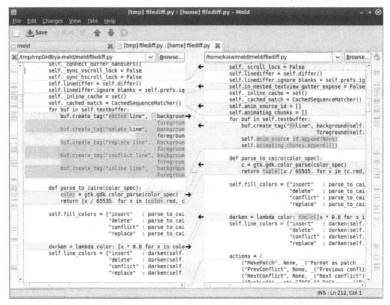

Meld is a graphical tool for comparing the contents of text files to determine what has changed. These tools can be used to great effect on CSV files to determine if a significant change has happened.
(Wikipedia:GNU License)

Techniques to Reduce the Problem

These are well-established problems, and well-established best practices are associated with them.

Compression

While not the focus of this article, compression is an easy and often overlooked solution to the problem. I am usually glad it is ignored from a solution architecture perspective. While putting the files in a zip archive is an easy solution, it does reduce the visibility of the changes: files need to be

198

decompressed before they can be compared. Compression should be maintained inside the solution and abstracted from the user.

Having users compress their files reduces the ability of tools to take other actions that may have a more significant impact.

Right-Scoped Repositories

In our initial problem description, the IT team had difficulty restoring the backups because they needed to fix the entire repository to a point in time.

Rather than creating backups of the entire repository (measured in petabytes for our example), breaking the problem down into sub-parts may be more sensible. Many of our projects will get archived over time, projects change at different rates, and usage may decline or increase. This means that some data will have a greater or lesser probability of requiring a restore at a given point in time.

Dividing the backups at a per-project level offers an obvious division point. This means that some data will have a greater or lesser probability of requiring a restore at a given time.

Only Store Changes

As discussed, tools like `diff` and `patch` offer a means to identify, store, and apply changes to larger files. Rather than storing multiple copies of the dataset, it is possible to store a primary dataset and then track the series of changes that have taken place on it.

For example, country lists change regularly, requiring an update for even a spelling change. A CSV based on the

Wikipedia page for ISO country codes could be modified with a patch description to accommodate Hungary's name change in 2012[54].

```
@@ -117,1 +117,1 @@
-Hungary,Hungary,UN member state,HU,HUN,348,.hu
+Hungary,Republic of Hungary,UN member
state,HU,HUN,348,.hu
```

This is significantly smaller than storing the entire file of hundreds of countries for a single name change. As a tip, the primary should be the one you are using, and the changes can work backwards.

A Solution

Rather than manually perform all of these steps, these are the problems that modern VCS applications were developed to solve. As an odd quirk of history, Subversion (SVN) is particularly well suited to handling large files as it only tracks the differences between states.

While I recommend any VCS solution as an improvement over file copies, SVN is ideally suited to Data Analyst's management of large datasets.

Take our original problem of a project storage system with archived folders.

---

[54] Statoids, Changes in ISO3166-1
http://www.statoids.com/w3166his.html

```
name                            size
----------------------------------------
/proj/1/
   schema.json                  128  B
   dashboard-template.html      232  KB
   dashboard.html               100  MB
   districts.csv                 37  MB
   postalcodes.csv               33  MB
   arch/
      dashboard.20220301.html   100  MB
      dashboard.20220315.html   100  MB
      dashboard.20220401.html   100  MB
      dashboard.20220415.html   100  MB
      districts.202203.csv       37  MB
      districts.202204.csv       37  MB
      postalcodes.202203.csv     33  MB
      postalcodes.202204.csv     33  MB
----------------------------------------
```

I have modified the example to include historic reports built from a template.

Rather than trying to retrofit, let's just start over (with project #2).

One of the first improvements we can make to the storage structure is creating an independent archive location for each project. This independent location can then be turned into an SVN-controlled location.

```
mkdir -p /arch/2;
cd /arch/2;
svnadmin create;
```

Now, we can link the archive location to the working area.

```
mkdir -p /proj/2;
cd /proj/2;
svn checkout file:///arch/2 .;
```

Once this is done, we can create our space and apply the changes as we make them.

```
name                            size
------------------------------------------
 /proj/2/
    schema.json                 128 B
    dashboard-template.html     232 KB
    dashboard.html              100 MB
    districts.csv                37 MB
    postalcodes.csv              33 MB
------------------------------------------
```

```
cd /proj/2;
svn add *;
svn commit -m "Change 2022-03-01";

copy /proj/1/arch/dashboard.20220315.html dashboard.html;
svn commit -m "Change 2022-03-15";

copy /proj/1/arch/dashboard.20220401.html dashboard.html;
copy /proj/1/arch/districts.20220401.csv districts.csv;
copy /proj/1/arch/postalcodes.20220401.csv postalcodes.csv;
svn commit -m "Change 2022-04-01";

copy /proj/1/arch/dashboard.20220415.html dashboard.html;
svn commit -m "Change 2022-04-15";
```

Under these conditions, you will create snapshots of the changes at each point something changed,

- Reducing the number of snapshots you have to maintain. No change, no snapshot

- Backups are generated per working folder, meaning if a restore is required, it only takes the size of the individual project to go back in time.

- Your backup footprint is reduced because SVN only stores the differences between each snapshot.

```
name                            size
----------------------------------------
 /proj/2/
   .svn/                        13.4 GB
   schema.json                   128  B
   dashboard-template.html       232 KB
```

```
    dashboard.html                    6.7 GB
    districts.csv                     5.0 GB
    postalcodes.csv                   1.7 GB

    ------------------------------------------------
```

Note the creation of the folder `.svn`, this is true for most VCS applications. They must create a control folder to track their link to the repository. Also, this folder will contain a single copy of the folder structure to allow it to detect changes, doubling the storage space in the short term. The total storage space in the working location remains untouched mainly as the changes are made.

Snapshots can be viewed via <u>SVN's log</u>[55] command.

```
$ svn log ^/ -qv
------------------------------------------------------------
r4 | jeff | 2022-04-15 00:43:13
Changed paths:
   M /dashboard.html
------------------------------------------------------------
r3 | jeff | 2022-04-01 12:25:08
Changed paths:
   M /dashboard.html
   M /districts.csv
   M /postalcodes.csv
```

And if a data restore needs to be performed for a user, it is simple to select the historical revision.

---

[55] Version Control with Subversion, v1.7, svn Subcommands
https://svnbook.red-bean.com/en/1.7/svn.ref.svn.c.log.html

```
mkdir -p /tmp/history;
pushd /tmp/history;
svn checkout -r 3 file:///arch/proj/2 .;
popd;
```

One final benefit is that because the archives are no longer stored with the working copy, a different type of storage can be applied to the backups. Slower storage can be applied to the backups, while faster storage can be used for the working copy.

The Social Aspect

Unfortunately, in many cases of this problem, I have seen the interested parties pointing at one another and saying it is the other person's fault. Data Analysts need to be made aware that version control tools exist. IT departments need to view backups and restores as more than whole-system-events for recovering from complete system failures.

The question becomes: who is this article designed for? Data Scientists or System Administrators.

This is really for both. Hopefully, both parties will work together to reduce costs and burdens on the other, but a change will likely have to start with the IT department.

Further, reducing costs is seen as a negative in most organizations. Cost is associated with prestige; managerial resumes often boast about the size of their budget. Reducing the budget reduces prestige.

A Scripted Solution

Given the social problems, the simplest means of introducing users is to implement a simplified Version Control practice in an **automated fashion** without asking users, offering training, or talking about it.

Two steps should be taken:

- Immediately install a VCS client on every computer that accesses the system in question

- Integrate VCS creation into the project allocation part of the process

On the project setup and allocation side, the process usually starts with a request for space on the computer as a paper form (yes, companies are still filling out paper forms, usually PDFs). As this kicks off a large process involving multiple configurations being manually configured, ensure the allocation of a VCS is part of that process. The simplest way to ensure this is done is to automate the entire process.

```bash
#!/bin/bash
proj="./proj";
arch="./arch";
function SetupFolder {
  f=$1;
  pPath="${proj}/${f}";
  aPath="${arch}/${f}";
  tPath=$(mktemp -d);
  mkdir -p "$aPath";
  svnadmin create "$aPath" && echo "Repository created." \
    || echo "Repository already exists ($?)";
  svn checkout "file://${aPath}" "$tPath";
```

```
    mv "$tPath/.svn" "$pPath/.svn";
    rm -rf "$tPath";
}
{
  proj=$(realpath ${proj});
  mkdir -p "$proj/00000000";
  echo "Project Folder: $proj";
  arch=$(realpath ${arch});
  mkdir -p "$arch";
  echo "Archive Folder: $arch";
  for dir in ${proj}/*/ ; do
    dir=$(basename "${dir}");
    echo "Updating: $dir" 1>&2;
    pPath="${proj}/${dir}";
    [[ -d "$pPath/.svn" ]] || {
      echo "  - linking project" 1>&2;
      SetupFolder "$dir";
    }
    pushd "$pPath";
    (( $(svn status | wc -l) > 0 )) && {
      echo "  - synchronizing changes" 1>&2;
      svn status | grep -e "^\?" | cut -c 9- | xargs svn add
{};
      svn status | grep -e "^\!" | cut -c 9- | xargs svn del
{};
      svn commit . -m "$(date -Iminutes)";
      svn cleanup;
    };
    popd;
  done;
} 1>/dev/null;
```

This script scans all folders and determines if a change has
been made. If there are changes, it submits them to the
archive location. If no archive location exists, it creates
one. This can be run on a timer, or better yet, can use

`inotify`[56] to monitor for changes. Better still would be to install a self-serve interface like GitLab that can auto-allocate space and control permissions[57], but ... bureaucracy.

Teaching Users

Secondly, an obvious VCS client should be installed on every computer in the office. By highly visible, I mean Tortoise on Windows[58][59] or RabbitVCS[60] on Linux. In both cases, the users are automatically presented with icons that tell them something unique about the folder to which they have been granted access.

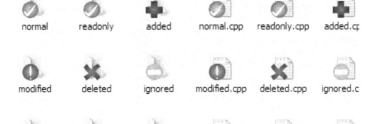

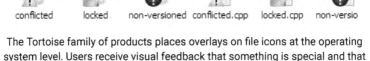

The Tortoise family of products places overlays on file icons at the operating system level. Users receive visual feedback that something is special and that they should learn more. (TortoiseSVN Manual, GPL)

---

[56] `inotify` man page. `inotify` can be used monitor for filesystem events
https://www.man7.org/linux/man-pages/man7/inotify.7.html
[57] DataLab is a GitLab configuration designed with Data Science workspaces in mind
https://gitlab.com/dpub/DataLab
[58] https://tortoisesvn.net/
[59] https://tortoisegit.org/
[60] http://rabbitvcs.org/

One of three things will happen:

1. A user already familiar with Change Management Systems will be pleasantly surprised

2. A user unfamiliar with Change Management Systems will curiously explore this new domain.

3. The user will not care... you can lead a horse to water, but you can't make it drink.

Once users see the log of the changes, they become aware that a history is kept for them, and they become empowered to restore their own historical data.

Once users see the log of the changes, they become aware that a history is kept for them, and they become empowered to restore their own historic data.

A Demonstration

To demonstrate how this all fits together, as well as to compare the compression capabilities of various setups, four versions of the script were created:

- CPY

  Makes a copy of the files in the project folders and sends them over to the archive location. This offers a baseline comparison of what our users are currently doing.

- FSZ

  The filesystem is compressed. We hope our users use ZIP, which creates a compressed copy of the folder each time the backup is called.

- GIT

  Git is an excellent VCS and should be included in any comparison.

- SVN

  The script that was offered earlier.

To simulate our users' activities, a script called `demonstrate.sh` downloads the history of the CIA World Factbook as JSON from GitHub, stores each change in the project folders and then backs them up. This is similar to our users receiving updates to their data files and then saving the old version to a backup folder. Results are stored in `results.csv`.

After 34 changes, <u>we can see</u> that Git and Zipped file systems perform almost equally, mainly because that is what Git does (zips of entire file structures); compression offers a lot of savings. By comparison, SVN shows almost no growth at all.

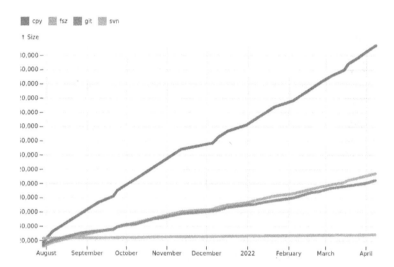

This brings us back to our original problem state: $70,000/year for storage, but using automated version control and SVN, in particular, we can reduce the storage costs by 90% to $7,000/year under real-world conditions.

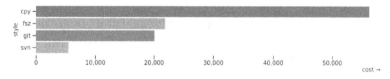

After 34 periods of change, SVN shows a significant cost savings (90%) over our original state.

That is a 90% cost savings, or about $63,000/year. In 2024, that is the wage of a Data Analyst for a year.[61]

---

[61]PayScale.com indicates a Data Analyst in Canada earns an average of 61,918/year, 2024-04-12

Most of these estimates are on the small side. Recent experience has shown the involved datasets to change in the 40G/quarter; suddenly, those numbers are in the millions of dollars.

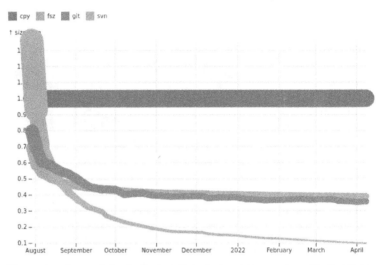

The cost savings, relative to the baseline storage, become more significant as time progresses.

Conclusion

This technique has been applied several times over the decades and has been demonstrated to work with not just text files but also Parquet and SAS data files in Tableau and RStudio applications.

Optimization of these techniques requires cognisant cooperation from both Data and System Analysts. Unfortunately, detailed information and change management techniques are not exciting and, therefore,

---

https://www.payscale.com/research/CA/Job=Data__Analyst/Salary

do not capture the attention of executives. However, a 90% decrease in costs (and consequently an increase in profits) should be addressed, and attention to these details is essential.

For this reason, I have presented these techniques using an automated but unobtrusive technique that fosters an environment that can encourage learning and cooperation.

Mostly, these techniques become necessary to reduce cost as an excuse for progress.

... because sometimes bureaucracy gets in the way.

As a final note, remember that cost correlates to carbon. Reducing your consumption is easily measured in dollars but also represents less pollution.

Save a byte, save the environment

How to Build a Simple In-Browser Search Engine

Because sometimes bureaucracy gets in the way.

- Addressing a Common Need: Create a simple in-browser search engine to manage a repository of organizational digital assets

- Overcoming Bureaucratic Hurdles: Explore using simple technology to overcome bureaucratic hurdles.

- Empowering User Accessibility: Simple tools significantly impact user accessibility, productivity and efficiency.

 A simple example working that indexes the CIA World Factbook, and then offer a search of the content. Search results offer a link to the actual page on the CIA's website.

Many years ago, I was asked to create a file repository for an air-gapped <u>conda repository</u>[62]. The idea was that, for security reasons, we would have a list of allowed libraries inside the costly secure environment and only those libraries. It was a <u>reasonably simple setup</u>[63], requiring only a large amount of storage and a simple static web server to deliver the files.

The simple filtered mirror allowed us to respond to user needs rapidly and quickly, adding or removing libraries from the secure environment. This meant the security team was much more willing to allow packages into the environment, knowing removing them would take hours rather than months or years.

- They were so thrilled we started using general search patterns to allow packages.

- We quickly went from dozens of packages to thousands.

- Users developed a new question to phone in and ask:

> **Which libraries are available?**

The list of libraries available was less than the official repositories but significantly larger than a human could

---

[62] Anacoda is a library repository and management system
https://anaconda.org/
[63] Conda Mirror is an Anaconda package for mirroring conda repositories
https://anaconda.org/conda-forge/conda-mirror

216

reasonably be expected to read through. It was also spread across several folders. All in all, it was just challenging to keep track of.

Users required a search engine like Anaconda.org, limited to our organisationally available packages.

An Aside

At this moment, in our story, I find myself away from home on business. Having attended an evening lecture in a pub in Gatineau, Quebec, on using technical systems to affect social change, and having had a few drinks, I found myself walking back to my hotel alone in the dead of a Canadian winter. Trying not to freeze to death and figure out where my hotel was, I started thinking about search problems. By the time I got back to my hotel, there was no way I could sleep, so I began to implement the solution.

Ahhh... the life of a programmer.

Unfortunately, bureaucracy got in the way. Getting the static HTTP server had been a feat of negotiation. To get the filesystem shared via HTTP, I had explicitly stated that this would only have static rendering turned on. This allowed us to skip undergoing months of security evaluations; no server-side processing meant no security risk to the network.

In order to accommodate both the need for a search engine and the lack of server-side processing, I built a simple search engine inside the browser.

Implementation

I have actually done this a couple of times before. In a few instances in my career, getting tools and computers have been significant barriers to a simple data processing engine. The key to this is that you can drop a simple HTML file at your server location, and it can then look up the data stored on the server.

Auto-index and Loading

 One requirement from the server is to ensure that some form of auto-index[64] is on. The server must advertise the available datasets to be processed so the client can discover they need processing. There are a couple of ways to achieve this; the simplest is to activate that feature on the server.

In similar systems, I have also used `bash` or `PowerShell` scripts to list all the datasets present: no information about them, just that they are present.

```
ls --format=single-column ./data/* > index.txt
```

The location of that file can then be passed to the script as its starting point for gathering all information.

---

[64] All static webservers have the ability to generate an index of content in a folder. In many cases servers may not have the feature on by default. In nginx, the module is called `ngx_http_autoindex_module` https://nginx.org/en/docs/http/ngx_http_autoindex_mo dule.html

218

```
const basePath = window.location;
const datasets = `${basePath}/index.txt`;
```

Once we have the list of data to be aggregated, we can begin the process of downloading, parsing, and storing.

Given we used PouchDB, we can immediately begin loading the text into the local database.

```
const db = new PouchDB('searcher');
async function LoadDB(){
    let recs = await fetch('./index.txt');
    recs = await rec.text();
    recs = rec.split('\n');
    for(let loc of recs){
      let content = await fetch(loc);
      let nRec = {
          _id: loc,
          text: nRec
      };
      let oRec = await db.get(loc);
      if(RecordsDiffer(nRec,oRec)){
          db.put(nRec);
      }
    }
}
```

The full text is now stored in the database for future use by the user. It is recommended that this be scanned periodically to see if any changes have occurred. (loader.js)

219

Sanitizing the Text

In database development and searching, an index can be considered a quick reference. In the days of manual searching, a card catalogue offered an alphabetic search ordered by subject, which allowed for a fast lookup. Rather than looking through every book in an entire building, you can look through a smaller listing in a single box.

Less is more, smaller is faster.

For this discussion, having a couple of documents we want to search will be helpful.

Fact 21

For every 25 percent increase in problem complexity, there is a 100 percent increase in complexity of the software solution. that's not a condition to try to change (even though reducing complexity is always a desirable thing to do); that's just the way it is.

Fact 22

Eighty percent of software work is intellectual. A fair amount of it is creative. Little of it is clerical.

— Robert L. Glass, Facts and Fallacies of Software Engineering

---

Our sample for discussion will revolve around indexing the text of Glass's Facts to allow for rapid lookup. It might be desirable to attach this to a microphone in the office, displaying an appropriate fact depending on what is being discussed (see chapter "The Angry Chatterbot").

Each fact can be placed in a separate record for our indexing to pick up later. This will allow us to treat each fact as a distinct entity.

```
./data/fact-01.txt
./data/fact-02.txt
./data/fact-03.txt
```

One issue with text like this is that a lot of it is meaningless or at least has low meaning. Some level of transformation should be performed to remove needless noise.

```
function sanitize(text){
    text = text.toLowerCase();
    text = text.replace(/[^a-z]/g,'.');
    text = text.split('.');
    text = text.filter(d=>{return d.length > 3;});
    return text;
}
let sanitized = sanitize(facts[21]);
```

As part of indexing fact number 21, we remove

- Case

- Non-text

- Short words (three characters, aka Stop Words)

Resulting in a sanitized list of words. (crepo.js)

221

```
[
'every', 'percent', 'increase', 'problem',
'complexity', 'there', 'percent', 'increase',
'complexity', 'software', 'solution', 'that',
'condition', 'change', 'even', 'though',
'reducing', 'complexity', 'always',
'desirable', 'thing', 'that', 'just'
]
```

The list can be further reduced by noting the duplicate words. A word count is a helpful way to weigh a term's value in a search.

```
function WordCount(list){
    let count = {};
    for(let word of list){
        count[word] = count[word] || 0;
        count[word]++;
    }
    return count;
}
let count = WordCount(sanitized);
```

Creating the Index

For this search, I chose to do a match on each word. This was done for simplicity and because it allows for searching for words that are out of order.

Examples of the kinds of searches I want a user to be able to use:

complexity	A word that is overly complex (it can be reduced to "complex")
ompl	A word that is partial match
Software olut	Multiple words
Solution software	Words out of order

These examples represent a couple of cases we need to handle. Most interesting is the partial match scenario.

To create an index, we need a list based on our lookup value that...

Key		Score	Document
database		100	<url>
atabase		99	<url>
tabase		98	<url>
abase		97	<url>
base		96	<url>
ase		95	<url>
databas		99	<url>
databa		98	<url>
. . .	. . .		. . .

... when you search for "data search", it finds ...

```
document    1
data        97
search     100
```

 ... for a total of 198 points, and then sorts by highest scoring documents (search.js)

Extras

Lemmatization

 As another layer, we can consider lemma[65]. Lemmatization refers to the most foundational word represented by a word. For example, "intellectual" can be thought of as being the same as "intellect". This will help reduce the number of possible typographic differences that occur later. For example, someone who remembers "that is" should find "that's". Come to think of it, "is" is a short word.

> every 25 percent increase problem complex there
> 100 percent increase complex software solution
> that condition change even though reduce complex
> always desire thing that just

---

[65] MichMech offers a simple lemmatization formats for use in analysis.
https://github.com/michmech/lemmatization-lists/blob/master/lemmatization-en.txt

This much simpler text version will reduce the amount of informational entropy (things that can go wrong in my head when remembering).

This text is well-sanitized and ready to undergo indexing.

Conclusion

The next morning, after writing the solution, I felt pleased with myself for having a complete solution that I could email to my primary customers (a few Data Science managers throughout the organization). I was so pleased that I showed it to a colleague who helped me optimize the index.

Years later, it is still the way the organization tracks available conda packages.

I could only pull this off overnight because I have implemented this so many times. I have used browser-side indexes to implement dashboards for regression testing, employee work allocation, personal blog searches, and a Project Gutenberg search engine. It even became the basis for a class I taught on Introductory JavaScript.

Since initially writing this, I have also discovered that the lead developer of PouchDB has written a full-text search[66]. You should use his solution, which is based on the lunr engine[67].

---

[66] PouchDB Quick Search, Nolan Lawson
https://github.com/pouchdb-community/pouchdb-quick-search
[67] Lunr is a javascript implementation of a Solr style search language
https://github.com/olivernn/lunr.js

Non-Optimal

This is not an optimal solution.

In this case, every search engine user must download and generate their own instance of the index. This requires the client to download the entire dataset the first time (increasing network traffic) for each browser they use.

In a case where I used this to build a regression testing dashboard, the initial download and parse of the test results took approximately 3 hours. Caching made it almost instantaneous if you kept up to date each day, but that first load was a big one.

One critical advantage of server-side processing is the ability to take the inbound data and generate the indexes once for all the customers. You could split the difference by generating the index on the server and having the clients download that constructed index. This would split the processing load between a central processor for the central data and distributed processing for the individual searches.

 This hints at an interesting balance between shared and distributed processing. Using databases that support the CouchDB[68] interchange protocol, each user can process new data as they find it and share the results back to a central pool used by the next person. This Lazy-Load form of data processing has some theoretical advantages (in a trusted environment). It would require very little central processing (expensive) and instead rely on existing

---

[68] CouchDB is the original Open Source database in the family of products, however there are several related and compatible products: CouchBase, CouchDB, PouchDB, CloudAnt
https://en.wikipedia.org/wiki/Apache_CouchDB

workstations. At the same time, it would share the workload to ensure no one computer took the brunt of the whole calculation.

Lastly, if this solution intrigues you, you should look into the Lucene-based searches provided for CouchDB, which are included with all commercial offerings.

228

Fishalytics

A (failed) experiment in data analysis as a behaviour modification tool

- Inefficiencies in daily life can act as an inspiration for social change.

- A simple record-keeping can evolve into a platform with social and ecological implications.

- Good ideas need good marketing to be successful. Social change requires social acceptance.

 Catch more fish by cooperatively tracking and sharing sport angling data (and improve ecological management at the same time)

Once upon a time, I gave up my 100-hour work weeks as a software developer, moved to the other side of Canada, and bought a small-holding farm. One of the first things I did when I moved to the new region was to buy a fishing license, and I was shocked when they handed me an official catch form with my license.

In the province I had moved to, when you have a recreational fishing license, you are expected to keep track of the number of fish you catch, the region you caught them in, and what species they are.

For a year.

I was struck by how inefficient this was. It was doubtful that I would remember *every* fish I caught for a year, and it was also unlikely that I would remember where I had put the fishing scorecard that I was required to send in at the end of the year.

A screenshot showing fishing licenses over the years. While I primarily fish in Canada, an acquaintance did give me written permission to fish in his private fishery in England. A fond memory to keep track of.

This seemed like a simple data entry form project that I might even be able to sell to the provincial government. At its simplest, the idea was that I could write an application that allowed fishermen to enter their fishing license information and record their fish as they caught them. At the end of the year, the software could print the scorecard for them.

Over the next 10 years, this tool became the focus of much of my internal pondering regarding system development and the ability of software to affect social change.

From Simple Record Keeping to Analysis

While the software's initial concept was to be a record-keeping tool for myself, it was only a short time before I started to think bigger.

1. If I built the tool, I could make it more widely available.

2. If I wanted others to use the tool, I needed to offer them more than just a fishing journal.

I had just hit on my first element of social design: you must offer something to the individuals you want to harvest data from. Like one of the major social platforms, I could harvest user data and sell it, but to do that, I first needed to offer something in return.

There were two value-added features I could think of right away.

1. The social aspect. Keeping pictures and memories of catching fish is fun. Sharing fishing tales in near

real-time would be a fun way for fishermen to engage with friends and a great way to record them for future memory.

2. Basic analysis. Knowing where you caught the last fish gives you some idea of where to catch future fish, and using aggregate data of many fishermen, I could offer solid, unbiased advice on where to catch the next fish.

That first idea that people could share was important; Facebook was young enough that competitive services were still reasonable in niche fields. Unfortunately, social platform development was really outside my domain of expertise. The second option spoke to my strengths, and it occurred to me that if I could develop a successful predictive product, partnering with a social partner could be performed later. Another benefit to focusing on the analysis was that I was the sole user at this point: building a social platform around a single individual is almost impossible; however, a single individual can gather multiple data points for analysis.

The first focus was set: predict what leads to catching more fish.

Planning the Data Gathering

In order to suggest to users what they should do to catch more fish, I first had to think of the variables that would impact the ability to catch fish. The best place to determine this was at my local lake, staring out over the water.

1. What about my fishing (behaviour) could affect my catching fish (outcome)?

2. Also, what could affect my ability to catch fish but was difficult to measure?

3. Lastly, what was easy to measure but probably had little to do with my catching fish (red herrings)?

In brainstorming these things, I came up with several things that greatly impacted my catch rate and were reasonably easy to measure.

- Location

- Time of Day (solar declination)

- Temperature (air and water)

- Solar penetration (cloud cover)

- Covering vegetation

- Lure

- Time spent fishing

- Time of Year

Unfortunately, only two seemed easy enough for the average fisherman (myself) to collect regularly. Space-time is easily captured on a phone, so anything involving those metrics is easy to capture: location, time of day, time of year, and solar declination.

These two items can be measured easily through smartphone GPS logging. By marking the start of a fishing trip and having the application continuously log the position of the person fishing, we can get a sense of how long they stood in a given location with a line in the water without catching fish. Upon catching a fish, it is natural to want to capture the moment. Snapping a picture (again through the app) marks the moment and location at which the fish was actually caught.

Measuring Success

Putting these variables together into a meaningful metric became the next problem.

We need a clear definition of success to determine which variables lead to success. To some extent, this requires distinguishing causal variables from outcome variables. To determine how a fisherman would consider themselves successful, there would be no better way than to interview a recreational fisherman.

I went fishing.

> You find gold where the gold is
>
> — Prospector's Proverb

Standing waist-deep in water at my local lake, with a line in the water, I began pondering the variables that would make me successful at that moment. As I stood there, I realized it was catching a lot of fish; catching fish is exciting, even small fish. So, there is an element of quantity. The sheer amount of fish you catch is a positive experience. But standing in a lake for 4 hours to catch two fish is not the same as hitting 2 fish in 20 minutes: the velocity at which we catch fish matters. At that moment, I caught the most impressive Small-mouth Bass I have ever caught. On a small fishing rod, a big fish is a fun experience. Fishermen brag about that giant fish they caught. So it's not only a measure of the quantity of fish caught, but also the quality of those fish.

A fishing trip can be measured as being successful by the velocity at which you catch fish.

$$velocity = \frac{quantity\ of\ thing}{time\ spent}$$

There is a little more to it, as we want to factor in the quality of the fish caught. We can also consider the entire time spent as a single fishing trip.

$$velocity = \frac{number\ of\ fish \cdot quality\ of\ fish}{time\ spent\ standing\ next\ to\ water}$$

The problem with this definition was that it needed to be more granular. The end goal was to create a heat map representing the best places to go fishing. This heat map would represent a range from null (no information) to good to bad. So, while a trip represents a range of space-time (different fish caught at different locations and times), I required highly granular data that specified a point in space-time.

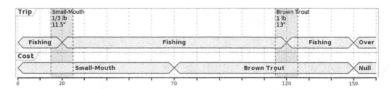

A hypothetical fishing trip with two fish caught. The fish took a certain
amount of time to catch which represents an effort on my part.

Here, we can take our cue from accounting. In addition to
the time when the success was achieved, we can measure
the time between as the cost of catching the fish.

In the example above, the Small Mouth only took 20
minutes to catch. However, I continued fishing without
seeing another for 50 minutes. We, therefore, allocated the
unsuccessful time to the nearest fish caught.

Given this new perspective, we can change the measure of
success to

$$score = \frac{quality\ of\ the\ fish}{time\ spent\ fishing\ for\ that\ fish}$$

While the trip score can be considered the average of all
the individual fish scores.

We are getting closer to a simple score with a clear
definition of how to measure the time per fish.
Unfortunately, the definition of a fish's quality is not
straightforward.

Generally, size is considered the measure of a successful
catch, but not all fish are considered equal. If I am fishing
in a mountain stream and catch a good-sized trout, it will

236

be a very different size from even a small Great White Shark. Age is also a factor: young fish will be smaller than older fish.

Another wrinkle that enters when we consider why the government was collecting this data is fisheries management. They want to know the health of the regional ecosystem. Under these conditions, it is not sufficient to understand that the fish is bigger but is an appropriate weight for its age. High or low values could indicate various stresses on the population.

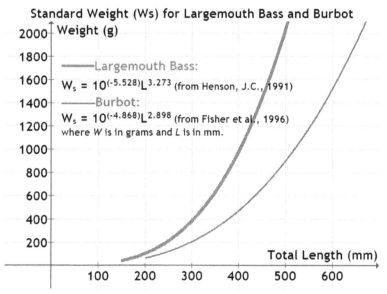

Standard Weight (Ws) for Largemouth Bass and Burbot

Weight (g)

Largemouth Bass:
$W_s = 10^{(-5.528)}L^{3.273}$ (from Henson, J.C., 1991)

Burbot:
$W_s = 10^{(-4.868)}L^{2.898}$ (from Fisher et al., 1996)
where W is in grams and L is in mm.

Total Length (mm)

Two Standard Weights for two different species. As length increases so does weight, but at different rates. (Wikipedia CCSA-3.0)

A species' Standard Weight is a measure of the average size of a fish given its height. This is basically BMI for fish: given a fish's length, we can consider its normal weight. This weight follows an exponential curve (fish get fatter faster than they get longer) and is unique to each species, with each species having two constants that define their normal curve.

To use this component of Standard Weights, a database of the a and b parameters for each species is required. Fortunately, that database exists in <u>Fish Base</u>[69], an online catalogue of fish research worldwide.

To identify a fish's parameters, all required is to know the fish species (a common name is acceptable) and the location where it was caught. This results in a page about a fish, including its Standard Weight. For example, our <u>Small Mouth Bass</u>[70]: (a) 0.0129, and (b) 3.06, (len) 8" or 216 mm, (weight) 1/3 lbs or 153g

---

a data | Bayesian analysis

ites are provided below, based on your selection of st jive less weight to studies that are far from the regres **netric mean a = 0.0129, mean b = 3.06, SD log10(V** gth: 0.0 (cm) = 0.00 (g) 95% range 0.00

The mean `a` and `b` values are offered in the footnotes.

Given this information, we can consider the quality of a fish to be its variance from its Standard Weight. Note that for convenience, scores are shifted to a positive range (catching a fish is always a good thing) between 0 and 1000 (because per mille has always amused me)

---

[69] FishBase is a global biodiversity information system on finfishes
https://fishbase.se/home.htm
[70] Smallmouth Bass Length Weight sampling from Fishbase
https://fishbase.se/popdyn/LWRelationshipList.php?ID=3382

```
stdWeight = StdWt(a,b,mm)
          = StdWt(0.0129,3.0600,203)
          = 156.3g

quality =   weight - stdWeight
            ------------------
                 stdWeight

        =   153g - 156.3g
            -------------
                156.3g

        =   -0.021113243762
```

for convenience, convert to per mille with 500% being the center point.

```
          = floor(-0.021113243762 / 2 + 0.5)
          = 489%
```

This should be further converted to the `score` by integrating the time spent fishing for the fish:

```
score = quality / time
      = 489 / 70
      = 7
```

Using the standardized quality method gives us a measure of the quality of each fish caught, allowing us to produce aggregate values (such as the trip score) without concern for species variability.

Analytics

By querying a space-time bounding box, a user can view places where fishing has been particularly good or bad. This was charted using OpenStreetMap, Leaflet.js, and Heatmap.js. It is useful not only for fishermen but also for ecologists looking to study the quality of the fish in the area.

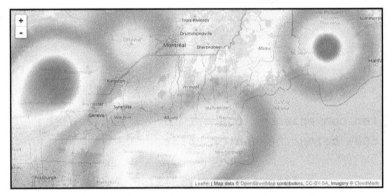

The default example from HeatMap.js (demo)

With sufficient observations, this standardization of the data allows for several other types of analysis

- Year-over-year analysis is possible, allowing ecologists to monitor for trends of declining or recovering populations.

- Species comparative analysis can show one species filling in for another species, a common symptom of an environment in distress.

- Time of day analysis, or seasonality, can improve catch rates by fishermen.

- Anonymously reported aggregated data encourages self-reporting of poaching.

This finally made me realize there were two additional target audiences for this data.

Fisheries Management

The ability to turn fishermen's stories into meaningful analytics meant fisheries didn't need to wait until the end of the season to get paper records. Real-time catch data collected by customers can be used to gain insight into the health of bodies of water. This means early interventions can be taken.

The Ecosystem

Fish populations are early warning signs of ecological disasters. Changes in the types and sizes of fish populations are a good indicator of the water's environmental health. These analytics provide real-time and early detection of ecological issues.

Fishermen don't want to fish in an overfished area, and ecologists don't want fishing in stressed areas. A system like this can help identify healthy fish populations and direct fishermen toward those, leaving stressed populations alone to recover.

Conclusion

FishAlytics was a failed social experiment for me. After nearly a decade, I abandoned the project without it ever moving past a personal fishing journal. Competing priorities (I was a farm labourer), legal obligations (I didn't want to lose intellectual property while working for some companies), and theft (a customer I pitched this to pitched it back to my students four years later) left me just not working on it and finally letting it go.

But it wasn't a waste of time either. It has offered me my first real introduction to the possibility of using Data Analysis as a tool for social change. Also, I started to conceive of how passive pressure could enact social change.

It also introduced me to the idea that everything can, and often should, be boiled down to a single health metric. This has been beneficial to me in other data analysis roles, where being able to identify variance in an abstract health metric has allowed for early intervention.

While I failed to achieve the desired results, I hope this article helps others see software and systems as more than forms on a page. Rather than simple forms, view them as tools for evolving social systems and modifying behaviour for the betterment of all.

Further Reading

There are a few libraries that are highly useful for this type of project

 Leaflet.js: a mapping library for interacting in the browser

 Plotly: a general charting library. Not used in the project, but a staple in things I do now

Heatmap.js: the library used for integrating heatmaps in FishAlytics

Also, if you want to enact social change through software development, there is a classic piece of work you must read.

 Wicked Problems: Problems Worth Solving: how do you implement social change in complex systems? This book addresses the problem.

Finally, while I have suggested valuable tools, with great power comes great responsibility. I, therefore, leave you with this warning from Charles Goodhart: Any observed statistical regularity will tend to collapse once pressure is placed upon it for control purposes, or more simply put ...

When a measure becomes a target, it ceases to be a good measure

— Goodhart's Law

244

Technologic (In)accessibility

Technology as a barrier to the beach

- Making assumptions about customer capability can create barriers to products.

- Technology itself acts as a barrier to entry for marginalized communities

- An analysis of the societal impact of technological accessibility issues emphasizes the importance of considering diverse user experiences in system design.

I went to the beach a couple of weeks ago.

Beaches are hard to come by on the bald Canadian prairies, so this was a rare treat for my wife and me. Having recently moved from a coastal city, we were looking forward to wading into some water and introducing our young dog to swimming. We had just learned about Sandy Point Beach in <u>Lacombe County</u>, were very excited and more than willing to spend a couple of hours in the car.

Upon arriving, an older gentleman wearing a security uniform informed us that parking had recently become paid parking (no problem) and that we just had to scan a QR code on a pamphlet he gave us (big problem).

I asked if the facilities offered free WiFi to connect to the payment service. I was assured there was plenty of service just up ahead. I tried to be specific that *I do not have a data plan* on my phone, but he did not seem to understand. I rolled the dice, proceeded in, found a parking spot, and attempted to pay: no WiFi. It did occur to me that it was closer to the change building, so I walked over to the building and tried there: no WiFi.

This was going to be a problem.

Upon returning to my car, I found the security guy had already taken my plate number. I did ask him what alternate options were available for me to pay. I did try to explain that I did not have any means to connect to the internet, but that only resulted in him getting frustrated with me and simply stating, you just open your phone, and you get the internet.

Unfortunately, this isn't true for everyone, and (as is often the case) assumptions regarding people's capabilities result in barriers to accessibility. These assumptions regarding customer abilities lead to not considering wheel-chair ramps, hazards not being demarked for the visually impaired, and audio tutorials not being offered to deaf people.

To some extent, assumptions are inevitable: not having lived a particular experience, it is natural to be unaware of the nuances involved in that experience. Fortunately, society is (mostly) aware that we are sometimes unaware of these physical barriers to entry, and we realize the importance of <u>seeking expert advice</u>[71].

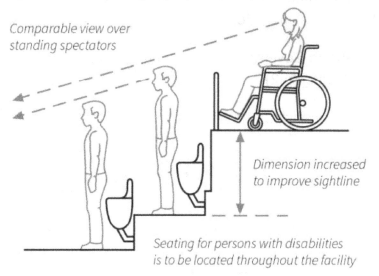

Comparable view over standing spectators

Dimension increased to improve sightline

Seating for persons with disabilities is to be located throughout the facility

There are subtle nuances and significant details that experts in a domain are aware of that are non-obvious to outsiders (p55, <u>Alberta Government: Barrier Free Design Guidelines</u>, 5th edition)

---

[71] Barrier-free design guide, Fifth edition, Alberta Government. Guides, such as this, represent the distilled knowledge of experts and are a good place to start https://open.alberta.ca/publications/barrier-free-design-guide-fifth-edition

Unfortunately, another set of barriers can be described as Technological Barriers, which are often not even considered. Due to marketing and the increased cost of implementation, technology is sold as simple to implement, which unfortunately overlooks some of the complex nuances of how humans interact with technology. We must be thoughtful in our design of technological and physical space.

> Thoughtful design means to consider how a space is to be used … The objective is to remove as many barriers as possible.
>
> — Alberta Government, <u>Barrier Free Design Guidelines</u> (p.2)

Accessibility of Technology

As users progress from discovering the service to seeking it out, many things can prevent them from engaging. We all know that technology significantly reduces these barriers: digitally readable text increases the options for consuming text, and networking allows communication to reach the consumer rather than the consumer coming to the message.

By diversifying our modes of communication, we create redundancies and alternate paths for our consumers to follow; these alternate paths allow those with various barriers to seek an alternate route to the same outcome.

One of the risks of easy and low-cost solutions is the temptation to use them to the exclusion of all else. This leaves no means for those with accessibility issues to bypass the barriers in their way ... and without personal experience, we will likely be unaware that those barriers exist. We need to rely on experts with domain knowledge to avoid making assumptions based on our expertise.

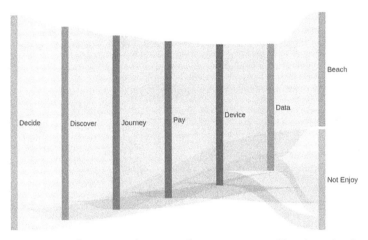

In any customer's progression toward success, several barriers slowly whittle away at those who can enjoy the product or service.

In this case, the assumption is that everyone has access to mobile devices and mobile data plans through one of the major Canadian providers. Unfortunately, this isn't true for 34% of Canadians[72], who, in a 2019 study, did not have access to a Smart Device. Many more do not pay for the internet to be accessible from their devices.

---

[72] Wait: 25% of Canadians still don't have ANY kind of mobile phone?, A Journal of Musical Things https://www.ajournalofmusicalthings.com/wait-25-of-ca nadians-still-dont-have-any-kind-of-mobile-phone/

This has changed during pandemic lockdowns, but there is still not complete coverage. <u>Statistics Canada observes</u> that 20% of Canadians do not have data plans on their mobiles as of 2021. This is even more pronounced among rural Canadians, at 27%, the very customers the rural county of Lacombe is trying to serve.

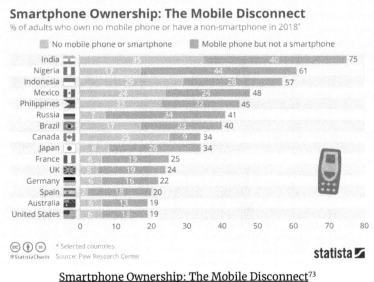

Smartphone Ownership: The Mobile Disconnect[73]

Cost of Technology

In the mid-2000s, the trend was toward shared WiFi and WiFi networks. This was a low-cost and ubiquitous solution to internet connectivity in urban areas (I loved my Nokia N800). As WiFi was ubiquitous in coffee shops and offices, many people never felt the need to purchase data plans.

---

[73] Smartphone Ownership: The Mobile Disconnect, Statista https://www.statista.com/chart/16937/share-of-adults-who-own-no-mobile-phone-or-have-a-non-smartphone

This is significant because, apparently, Canadians pay a lot[74] for their mobile data—among the World's most expensive[75] rates. In Canada, it is not unreasonable for a couple to pay $1800-$2500/year for internet connectivity on their phones, which cost $720-$1200/year[76].

If the average income of a couple in Lacombe County[77] is about $82,000/year, a total data cost of $3700/year represents a significant proportion (4.5%). Considering the considerable acceleration of inflation in Canada, leading to an 8.1% inflation rate[78] in 2020, one can foresee that Canadians will be seeking means to reduce their household expenses, and a 4.5% budget item, with an easy workaround (public WiFi) is an obvious candidate for cost

[74] Do Canadians pay too much for internet and cellphone service?, CBC News
https://www.cbc.ca/player/play/video/1.6522869
[75] 'Worst in the world': Here are all the rankings in which Canada is now last, National Post, 2022-08-11
https://nationalpost.com/news/canada/worst-in-the-world-here-are-all-the-rankings-in-which-canada-is-now-last
[76] Telus and Shaw Mobile Phone Plans, 2020
https://www.telus.com/en/mobility/plans
https://www.shaw.ca/internet/plans/
[77] Household income statistics by household type: Canada, provinces and territories, census divisions and census subdivisions
https://www150.statcan.gc.ca/t1/tbl1/en/tv.action?pid=9810005701&pickMembers%5B0%5D=1.4275&pickMembers%5B1%5D=2.4
[78] "Inflation rate will remain 'painfully high' all year, Bank of Canada governor anticipates", CTV News, 2020-07-21
https://www.ctvnews.ca/politics/inflation-rate-will-remain-painfully-high-all-year-bank-of-canada-governor-anticipates-1.5995379

reduction.

Canada is currently experiencing unprecedented inflation at 8.1%. Since early 2021, inflation has been accelerating[79]

... and that is not even the group we are concerned with.

When designing a system with an eye to accessibility, it is essential to consider those outside the norm. Having an average or above-average income represents a privileged group of decision-making individuals. It's easy to forget that about 16% of the population is financially vulnerable.

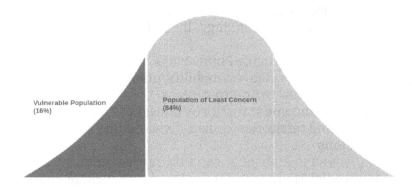

---

[79] Inflation Control Target, Bank of Canada, 2020. Red annotations added for emphasis.
https://www.bankofcanada.ca/rates/indicators/key-varia
bles/inflation-control-target/

In the case of governmental resource management, it is important to consider the less advantaged and vulnerable populations of the community. A day at the beach represents an attractive, cost-effective activity for low-income and vulnerable individuals (retired pensioners, single parents, or those who have just fallen on hard times). Socially, these people are best served by having access to public resources. At the same time, they are also the most vulnerable to having to make hard budget decisions.

Table Topping

When designing a technological system, it is essential to walk through the proposed system to identify potential vulnerabilities. While this walk-through <u>should be done in the actual environment</u>, it is worth doing as a <u>tabletop exercise</u>[80] in its early stages.

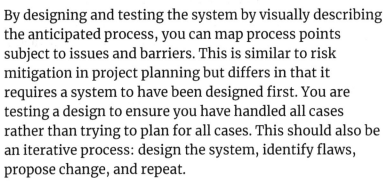

By designing and testing the system by visually describing the anticipated process, you can map process points subject to issues and barriers. This is similar to risk mitigation in project planning but differs in that it requires a system to have been designed first. You are testing a design to ensure you have handled all cases rather than trying to plan for all cases. This should also be an iterative process: design the system, identify flaws, propose change, and repeat.

---

[80] "Tabletop exercises explained: Definition, examples, and objectives", Josh Fruhlinger, 2024-04-02 https://www.csoonline.com/article/570871/tabletop-exer cises-explained-definition-examples-and-objectives.ht ml

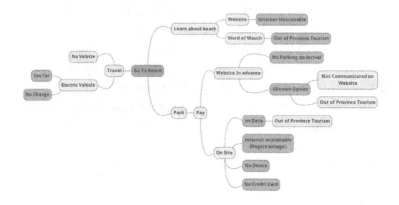

A quick mind-map addressing potential negative outcomes that should
be addressed

These issues and barriers can be documented and
considered for the probability of occurrence, impact
significance, and mitigation plan. Only some things need
to be handled, but they should be acknowledged.

Scenario	Issue	Prob	Sev	Mitigation
Park-Pay-Onsite-Website	No Data	20%	High	Kiosk
Park-Pay-Onsite-Kiosk	Not Exist	20%	High	-
Park-Pay-Onsite-Website	Bad Network	1%	High	Free Day

It is very common in this process to have our bias show
through and to be dismissive of an issue that is difficult or
uncomfortable to address or sometimes challenges our
worldview (eg. I have the internet on my phone, everyone I
know has internet on their phone. Therefore everyone has
internet on their phone). This is most dangerous at

executive levels, as <u>off-hand remarks may communicate</u>[81] decisions and desires to analysts and designers (having opinions is normal, but voicing them can be dangerous).

Conclusion

Having walked through the case, we can see how important it is that organizations approach their system design with an eye to accessibility and take active measures to prevent analyst and executive privilege from creating a bias that excludes the vulnerable. We can also see some tools used to mitigate and manage these issues.

Unfortunately, this particular technology implementation to support parking payments at Sandy Point Beach has made the beach inaccessible to many people. While I understand and agree that the county should be charging some fee to offset the creation of an artificial beach in the middle of The Prairies (I saw the mountain of sand off to the side), having no onsite means of payment available to patrons (WiFi, cash kiosk, or digital kiosk) means that what should be an affordable, and accessible, form of entertainment for residents, and tourists, has an insurmountable technological and financial barrier for many.

Lacombe County indicates that this trial run focused on education, so no tickets were issued. They also note that

---

[81] Thomas Becket was killed by King Henry's knights when, in a moment's rage, he said, "What miserable drones and traitors have I nurtured and promoted in my household who let their lord be treated with such shameful contempt by a low-born clerk!". That off-handed comment, sparked a murder, a revolt, and nearly cost him the throne.
https://www.britishmuseum.org/blog/thomas-becket-murder-shook-middle-ages

payment can be made in advance at the County Office or online. However, neither option is mentioned on their website. Perhaps this is an exercise in table-topping, and they have taken the time to consult the appropriate experts.

Unfortunately, this demonstrates how we (as decision-makers) can fail to identify these issues as we rely on our own life experiences and fail to be aware of the diverse experiences of others. We can fail to address the problems in advance or create viable alternative success paths.

In the end, it was a frustrating start to what was supposed to be an exciting day for my wife, myself, and my dog. It has turned a public resource into a technologically accessible one only for the privileged.

Healthcare professionals say that dangerous heat puts marginalised and vulnerable communities at risk because low income populations have a more difficult time accessing cooler spaces and green-spaces

— Millions of Canadians try to stay cool during heat wave, CBC, 2022-08-12

Paper as a Digital Storage Medium

Distributing Data in the Present and Preserving Data for the Future

- Describes the concept of utilizing paper as a digital storage medium

- Combine the reproducibility of digital data with the long-term storage capabilities of paper.

- Explore the challenges of modern information distribution and preservation, including the risks of centralized data storage and the loss of historic copies.

 An experiment in using barcodes as a storage medium. Create an EPUB reader that stores its data on paper.

Two Stories

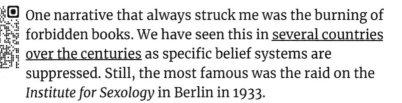 A story about anonymity

In recent times, we have seen a war of information. In Russia, <u>news sources are being silenced</u>[82] for criticizing their invasion of Ukraine. In China, online speech is monitored and can result in <u>punitive damages</u>[83] for individuals. Saudi Arabia asks neighbours to denounce each other.

My grandparents migrated from Europe to North America after WWII. Europe had troubles after the war, and, as with so many other refugees, everything my grandparents possessed had been lost, so a move to a new land filled with opportunities captured their imaginations. I grew up on stories my Grandmother and various Aunts passed down to me, which inspired me to read more.

One narrative that always struck me was the burning of forbidden books. We have seen this in <u>several countries over the centuries</u> as specific belief systems are suppressed. Still, the most famous was the raid on the *Institute for Sexology* in Berlin in 1933.

---

[82] "More Russian media outlets close as Moscow cracks down", Anna Cooban, CNN Business, 2023-03-04 https://www.cnn.com/2022/03/04/media/russia-media-crack-down/index.html

[83] "Hong Kong's Crackdown on Dissent Hits Facebook Pages", Newley Purnell, Wall Street Journal, 2022-08-16 https://www.wsj.com/articles/hong-kongs-crackdown-on-dissent-hits-facebook-pages-11660645491

The *Institut für Sexualwissenschaft* was the leading organization dedicated to the study and advocacy of alternate sexuality in Europe. On May 6th, Government Officials raided the facility. Much of the early research (and advocacy) of gender studies was dragged out into the streets and dramatically destroyed for being un-German.

When people first learn of the story, they are rightly distressed about the knowledge that was forever lost. Still, a lesson is learned from the later stories of lost treasure troves being recovered from someone's basement after the war. Here is how the story goes in my head.

Magnus Hirschfeld publishes a great work and gives all his students copies. The professor and his students are arrested and executed, and their personal libraries are looted and destroyed. Fortunately, Li Shiu Tong, one of his students, had lent the book to an acquaintance. The acquaintance

> was sympathetic to the NSDAP authorities but did not want to cause trouble for his friend. He had put it on his bookshelf and forgotten about it. Years later, when he died, his wife put all the books into boxes and stored them in the attic, where they stayed for the next 50 years because nobody was looking for a forgotten book in a forgotten collection.

In my internal narrative, this happens on the East German side, where Stalin continued to suppress homosexuality. The book is completely lost, except for that one accident in which it was put away in a box and forgotten about. It has a chance at a new life when society is ready for change.

The ability to be forgotten and anonymous is significant in disseminating dissenting opinions.

In the modern era, as information delivery systems have become more robust, we see the same destruction of knowledge taking place, though more subtly. As the distribution cost has been reduced, we have seen data become centralized: it is much easier to visit Wikipedia on your phone than to download the page and carry it around. Also, Wikipedia has an open edit history associated with the documents; not all websites are so open.

This leads to two risks:

1. There is the risk of the lone copy in a single organization's archive and content being removed from the library (webserver). In the example above, Hirschfield indicated that his library should be donated to the University if the Institute is closed. This never happened; the forced closure was deemed legal, and all copies were destroyed.

2. This centralization means that content can be edited without maintaining historical copies. Since the edit history is lost, it can never track significant shifting of opinions. History can be changed.

The Internet Archive[84] demonstrates[85] the need for this: websites and content are regularly removed from the Internet for reasons as innocuous as cost (part of the reason Git was developed was to protect OSS from being lost to public servers being shut down) and as nefarious as governments shutting down news stations[86] to silence dissent. Central repositories like the Internet Archive help to protect knowledge by allowing us to observe changes, but they also put knowledge at risk by being the only keepers of history.

Distributing the data across many bookshelves protects it from complete loss.

A story about storage

Many years ago, I heard a story. I don't know if it is true, but it carries a valuable lesson.

---

[84] Building Democracy's Library, Internet Archive Blogs, Chris Freeland, 2022-09-06
https://blog.archive.org/2022/09/06/building-democracys-library-celebrate-with-the-internet-archive-on-october-19/
[85] An Egyptian Perspective on American Book Banning, Hassan Said, Internet Archive Blogs, 2022-03-10
https://blog.archive.org/2022/03/10/guest-blog-an-egyptian-perspective-on-american-book-banning/
[86] More Russian media outlets close as Moscow cracks down, Anna Cooban, CNN, 2022-03-04
https://www.cnn.com/2022/03/04/media/russia-media-crack-down/index.html

In the early '90s, an amazing product became accessible that allowed people to generate a lot more data than they ever had and of a higher quality than ever before: Microsoft Word. What had previously been stored on paper could now be digitally encoded and stored on disk. The archivists loved it; they were stuffing data onto disks left, right, and centre.

In the late '90s, Microsoft upgraded Word.

Into an incompatible format.

There was no way to recover all that long-term stored data. Legally, they were not allowed to, as it had to be stored exactly as it was placed into storage (and signed off on).

In another twist, magnetic storage degrades over time and is subject to limited environmental conditions. It is very easy to damage the storage medium.

In the story I was told, Archivists at the US Congressional Library said, "You know what doesn't degrade? Paper." They promptly started printing everything to paper, bundling it, and storing it in the existing vaults.

What if there was a way to have the best of both worlds? What if it is possible to have the fidelity of digital storage with the lifespan of paper, the volume of transmission available in Smart Devices, and the anonymity of in-person conversation?

Unfortunately, much of the data produced now is *dynamic*. By dynamic, you can interact with the visualization itself (scroll through a map, rotate a 3D model, filter, search, and aggregate massive datasets), but once it has been printed to paper, that is no longer possible.

Also, it takes a lot of work to transfer large data tables from paper to digital media. Scanning the documents as images and using OCR to collect tables of information loses significant amounts of metadata:

- Data Types must be guessed from the content

- Alignment issues cause data to be considered out of context

- Character fidelity can cause incorrect values to be interpreted

While high-resolution photography and Artificial Intelligence have certainly improved the quality of scanned content, the data is still transferred analogueically, which can result in mistakes.

Defining the Problem

What if there was a way to compromise between the two worlds: the long-term storage of paper, with the high fidelity of digital; the anonymity of a private conversation, and the distribution capacity of a computer network?

We are looking for a means to store digital information on physical media such as paper or etched into stone. We might call this visible media.

Properties of Digital

Companies, governments, and individuals have a desire to store data for long periods for legal archival purposes. This is hard to do. Over the past 20 to 30 years, digital storage costs have reduced as we moved from paper to magnetic storage. This presents a problem for archivists who must store the resulting volumes of data. As it becomes cheaper for us to produce data, it becomes a greater challenge for archivists to store it.

The data must have a simple interpretation: it must be stored in a format easily converted to something a human can read. Open Source standards are advantageous as they are unencumbered by intellectual ownership and are readily understood by a larger pool of experts.

Copying digital data is something we take for granted. When we make a copy of digital data, it is an exact copy. For example, music loses some fidelity when recorded in a high-resolution format; however, the replication of the song from that point forward retains an exact copy (at the resolution of the bit).

Properties of the Storage Media

While etching into stone or carving into wood are viable options, the weight and volume of these media present a barrier to storage space and weight. Linen and cotton sheets represent lighter options but are expensive to produce. Mylar and projector film reduce the size, which offers good potential.

Modern archival paper represents a balance of permanence, weight, and volume. Each of these could (and should) be considered for various purposes; the solution should be adaptable to all these solutions. We discuss paper as the primary media because paper has such a rich evolutionary history as a storage media.

A digital storage mechanism must offer a reasonable level of compression. By compression, we refer to the number of bits of information stored per square inch or pound. This means it should be able to keep the record in a physically small space, though this must be balanced with the ability to read it back easily.

Solution

Combining the needs of both these mediums allows us to integrate existing technologies to create a unique solution. ePUB is an Open-Source container format[87] for Electronic Books that offers a standardized[88] and unencumbered format for many data types. Further, 2D barcodes (in the form of QR Codes) have become ubiquitous to transmit URLs. However, fundamentally, they are just binary buffers capable of storing any encoded sequence of numbers.

ePUB

- Diverse data storage

- Compression

- Accessibility Conformance

- Widely Consumable

The transition from paper publishing to screen-based mediums brought some transitional challenges. PDF was popularized to digitize paper and act as an intermediary between paper and digital formats. On the polar opposite end of the spectrum from paper, digitized standards (such

---

[87] EPUB 3.3, W3C Recommendation
https://www.w3.org/TR/epub-33/
[88] ISO/IEC TS 30135-1:2014. Information Technology – Digital publishing - EPUB3
https://www.iso.org/standard/53255.html

as those developed by the W3C) have been optimized for delivery to an unknown display.

HTML introduced the idea of reformatting content to adjust to meet the consumer's needs. This meant that the text could be read by a screen reader, could reflow for people reading on small screens, or could be made more significant for people with poor eyesight. This accessibility of the format gave birth to a plethora of other standards now managed by the W3C. These standards ensure maximum availability to the most significant number of consumers.

ePUB takes advantage of these standards to encapsulate websites into a single document. They embed webpages into a ZIP file format to allow for the contained viewing of the entire website. Generally, the documents are organized into Chapters.

Anyone can read and decode a digital document using the common ePUB format. ePUBv3 allows for JavaScript to be embedded, meaning you could embed maps, interactive diagrams, etc. (like R-shiny, but self-contained). As a general W3C container, it is possible to embed other file formats for consumption and preservation: datasets as CSV or evidence in the form of video.

Barcodes

You can encode digital information into barcodes, which can then be printed to paper for long-term archiving, and the barcodes can be read back to a digital device for reading.

2 Dimensional barcodes have been used for decades to encode specialized information. BRML[89], text, or other data formats have been appended to printed documents, such as Driver's Licenses and invoices, to supplement the text with digital information. This usually amounts to a unique document identifier or a digital record.

Encoding an ePUB should be trivial, with there being several issues:

1. The encoding scheme must be identifiable by a reader (there must be sufficient information embedded in the data to allow a reader to reconstruct the correct form)

2. The size of a single book will likely exceed a given 2D barcode's storage capacity. An encoding mechanism will have to be able to span multiple image tiles.

3. A social issue must be managed because humans cannot read the codes directly. It is possible that they do not wish to view the material for legal, religious, or moral reasons. There must be sufficient metadata to allow the viewer to decide not to accept the message.

Once identified, the issues are easily overcome; adding metadata to the individual tiles in the application identifier, pagination, title, author, and subject should offer sufficient information to allow users to interact with individual tiles and reconstruct the data.

---

[89] Business Rules Markup Language (BRML), Cover Pages - Technology Reports, 2002-11-05
https://xml.coverpages.org/brml.html

A prototype of the concept has been created to demonstrate the capability. The prototype's protocol consists of

1. **A URL**: which points to the reader for either online use (browser only) or installation as a PWA, or just as a unique identifier that this is a compatible format.

2. **A Protocol Version**: as changes are made, the correct decoder must be used.

3. **Pagination**: the current tile number and the total number of tiles to be converted. This allows for correct sequencing as well as a measure of progress.

4. **Bibliographic**: Title, Author, and subject allow readers to decide if this content interests them or is legal for them to interact with. Filters can be added to prevent accidental downloads from taking up space.

5. **Parental Rating:** not so much for parents, but generally for people that are not interested in certain types of content (filtering `xxx` content from a work device, for example)

6. **Relevance Date**: Some content is only valid up to a certain point and should be ignored after that (e.g., a poster for a concert). Offer a hint to the reader that perhaps this could be removed or ignored.

With this information in every tile, the read of the first image can result in some information being given to the user, allowing them to decide whether to continue or block. If they choose to continue, pagination can be used to determine the order in which the buffers should be ordered for reconstruction.

A prototypic specification is <u>available in more detail</u>[90].

Various Uses

Secure Archives

Having access to an archive comes with permission issues. Controlling access to information in archives that store sensitive data can be difficult. Using this encoding mechanism acts as an envelope around the content.

In the description of meta-data, the content rating was suggested. Reusing this protocol portion to use classification ratings would be very easy. Users offered access to a secure document could have their specialized reader check the content's classification rating before decoding it. Suppose the individual only has <u>sufficient clearance</u> to view some related documents. Still, some of the papers in the area contain information that exceeds the individual's current clearance. In that case, it can be a secondary filter for viewing it.

Obviously, this would be a tool to assist honest actors within the environment and not a way to interfere with malicious actors. Still, it is another layer of protection that helps the actors manage the information they possess.

---

[90] Barcode EPub specification – draft
https://gitlab.com/dpub/barcode-epub/-/wikis/Specs/Blocks

Information Dissemination

Assuming you are in a place where information is controlled, you could print essays and newsletters on paper, which can be scanned for later reading. For example, it could be printed in a pamphlet or posted on a bulletin board, and nobody would know who published it (<u>beware of barcodes hidden on printouts</u>).

One of the advantages, in this case, is the high compression ratio. In an early test, a hundred-page novel was compressed to 9 pages of barcodes. While still requiring some effort to distribute, the entirety of the novel could be tacked to a corkboard.

The contents would then convert to something readable on your phone, like an inspirational poster.

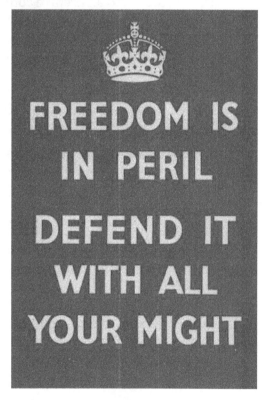

FREEDOM IS IN PERIL DEFEND IT WITH ALL YOUR MIGHT

Remote Interactive Media

Textbooks, posters, and advertising all have the common element of having to display content in physically contextual locations: a sign in a museum or a poster stapled to a lamppost. Without access to network communications, the audience misses out on an opportunity.

Take, for example, a sign at the top of a mountain congratulating a mountain climber on their successful journey. A digital experience message could be left at the top, but it would require configuring and powering a WiFi-based website.

Alternatively, storing the immersive experience directly on the poster would allow the digital content to be available but not require any power for maintenance.

In such circumstances, etching the information into something more permanent, such as wood or stone, may be appropriate. The Judaculla Rock shows carvings from 2000BC demonstrates the staying power and low maintenance capabilities of etching into stone.

Conclusion

Anonymous and long-term storage of data and information is necessary. The free dissemination of ideas and their storage for future reference is fundamental for society's progress. While the digital age has made information more accessible than ever, it has also introduced many new problems.

Using paper as a digital storage medium is a novel and valuable approach to addressing some new problematic circumstances.

Further Reading

The Internet Archive, <u>Digital Books wear out faster than Physical Books (November 15, 2022)</u>

 NYU Law, <u>The Anti-Ownership Ebook Economy</u>

How Publishers and Platforms Have Reshaped the Way We Read in the Digital Age

Storing Data in QR Codes

Encoding data on physical media for Dummy Programmers

- Innovative concept: Explores encoding data on physical media, using QR codes.

- Step-by-step tutorial: Provides clear instructions and visuals for storing digital data as an image, accessible even to beginners.

- Further exploration: Hints at advanced techniques and practical applications, serving as a comprehensive guide for interested readers.

In the last chapter, we looked at the benefits of storing data on physical media, including long-term storage capacity, publisher anonymity, and distribution privacy. The question that was not answered was, how do you do it?

Computers are computers, and use disks and files... how would you manage to store digital information on paper!?

This idea first occurred while teaching introductory programming at my local community college. I was looking to find people interested in using computers for social justice and trying to find ways to change the world. The idea was to put posters around the school with an invitation to a Data Analysis club, but they were encoded so that only interested students would spot them.

While those days are behind me, passing secret messages just to those who have eyes to see still sounds like fun.

A simple demonstration is probably the easiest... it certainly is the most fun. I encourage you to play along.

How do you store digital as an image?

Remember when you were in grade school, and your teacher separated you from your friends so you couldn't talk to one another? You created a secret code with your friend and started passing notes.

We are going to create a secret message to pass on to a friend.

Pre-Requisites

- A sample file

- A hex editor

- Some Grid Paper

- A pencil, eraser and scissors

Going through this exercise with a friend might be fun. It's like passing secret messages around the class in elementary school.

Inspect the file

Open your sample file with a hex editor. You should see something like this...

```
|50 4B 03 04 14 00 00 08 00 00 25 30 8B 51|PK........%0.Q|
|6F 61 AB 2C 14 00 00 00 14 00 00 00 08 00|oa.,..........|
|00 00 6D 69 6D 65 74 79 70 65 61 70 70 6C|..mimetypeappl|
|69 63 61 74 69 6F 6E 2F 65 70 75 62 2B 7A|ication/epub+z|
|69 70 50 4B 03 04 14 00 00 08 08 00 25 30|ipPK........%0|
|8B 51 00 00 00 00 02 00 00 00 00 00 00 00|.Q............|
|09 00 00 00 4D 45 54 41 2D 49 4E 46 2F 03|....META-INF/.|
|00 50 4B 03 04 14 00 00 08 08 00 25 30 8B|.PK........%0.|
|51 90 9F 06 74 9A 00 00 00 F4 00 00 00 16|Q...t.........|
```

Most people don't bother inspecting the actual contents of files (HINT: That's why people prefer data transfers as text). Still, you can get a lot of exciting information by bypassing the computer programs designed to use them.

For example, with a bit of know-how, we can immediately tell two things about the file we have open:

1. It is probably a `zip` file

    The first two bytes of the file are the values **50** and **4B** (in hex notation). Interestingly, these values correspond to the **ASCII** characters **PK**. Many years ago, signing the start of your application's files became customary to tell your files apart from other formats. **PK** stands for PKZip by PKware, the original company that created the file format.

2. It is an **epub** file

    Secondly, we can see that the `mimetype` is `application/epub+zip`. So, it's an EPub file (and confirmed as a zip).

There is a lot of information at the binary level.

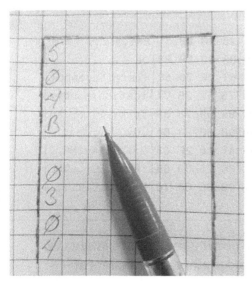

Serialise

The goal is to convert the file to a readable format. The easiest way to do this is to convert one byte at a time.

This has the advantage of doing it in order. Order matters, so by reading from the start to the end in order, we ensure that the person we send the message to gets it correctly.

So let's read the first byte, it is the hexadecimal value **50**.

Write that down on your grid paper (and maybe the next couple of values while we are at it)

Convert to Binary

We are looking for a sequence of bits; each hex digit represents 4 bits (half a byte or a nibble). So, we need to convert each digit to its binary form.

Taking the first one:

- 5_{16}

- 5_{10}

- 0111_2

Don't be afraid to use your computer's calculator.

Because this is a secret note, we need to remove our original working numbers. Grab your scissors and cut the first column off the paper.

(I'm switching my notation to ASCII art... for those who want to play along in a text editor)

```
------  ------
_0101_  _0000_
_0000_  _0011_
_0100_  _????_
_1011_  _????_
------  ------
```

Convert to Image

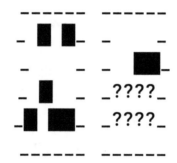

A barcode is just an image that can be interpreted as numbers. The key for us is that we don't have to use the symbols 0 and 1; any two easily distinguishable symbols would work just fine.

This is similar to how Morse Code works, in which a binary sequence of characters is represented by different lengths of tones. What is used doesn't matter as long as the two things are distinguishable.

One really good symbol easily distinguishable by a computer with a camera would be `light` and `dark`. This is convenient because colour can easily be printed on paper. We can use "the absence of pigment" (light) to represent 0 and "the presence of pigment" to represent 1.

Remember how I said to use a pencil?

1. Take your eraser, and erase every 0

2. Take your pencil, and colour every 1

My Eyes Are Buggy

This is coming along nicely. We now have a series of binary digits encoded as bars of colour. This is also known as a barcode.

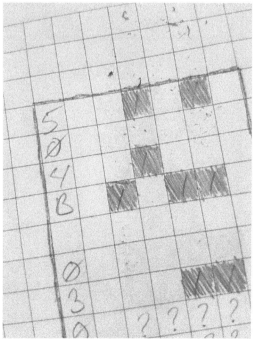

There's still one problem.

I'm getting old.

My eyes aren't what they used to be.

It's hard for me to follow where the lines start and stop.

This is especially problematic on lines with nothing in them at all. The number zero (line number 2) has no mechanism to show that it is a zero. To help our friend who needs to decode our secret message, let's put some guidelines in place. This will help them see where lines start and stop or if there is a line at all. The decoder also needs some way to know how big the squares are to help distinguish where digits start and stop.

You will notice I left some placeholders in my notation; let's fill them in:

1. Colour all the blocks down the left

2. Colour every other block across the top

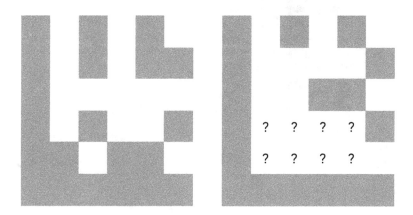

These guides tell where blocks start and how big each bit square is on the paper.

Huh... that looks an awful lot like a 2-D barcode.

Homework

Considering an ANSI-character table and considering bytes come in 8-bit sets, it is probably a little easier to write the blocks in **8x8** grids:

— *Susan Blackmore*

Extra: Parallel Delivery

You will notice that with these guidelines in place, we can treat each 8x8 grid as a separate block to decode. This makes it a little bit easier on us mentally, as well as offering another way to make our message easier to decode by the receiver:

1. On the back of each block, write its sequence number.

2. Cut-out each block

When your receiver gets all the blocks, they can share the work with some helpers. Each person can encode their little block, and the blocks can be stitched back together later.

Further Reading

It is time to point out that this is a *simplified* example. This was a demonstration that such a thing is possible.

When going from nothing to something, the first step is understanding that it's possible. Now that you know that such a thing is possible, it's time to go on to the insane ways to make it better:

 The Unicode Miracle One of the big problems with the above solution to the barcode problem is the number of wasted bits. Take a look at Unicode to see how much information can be packed into a bit.

 Wikipedia: Datamatrix Once you get your head wrapped around that, consider DataMatrix and how it packs more data into the same space.

 (then just know that there is an actual spec to conform to GS1 Datamatrix Specification)

 1D, 2D, and 3D Barcodes Now have your mind blown by 3D Barcodes. (For the record, I reject 4D Barcodes as a matter of principle)

If you are interested in a practical application and this just whets your appetite, I encourage you to check out Barcode Epub, a barcode-to-epub converter suitable for anonymous transfer and archiving of everything from

Digital Marketing posters to publishing data used in your thesis.

Maybe you can even pin it to a message board.

The Angry Chatterbot

A (successful) experiment in software as a behaviour modification tool

- Using software to modify inappropriate social behaviour in virtual environments through negative feedback.

- Managing social dynamics within teams is challenging, especially where communication is crucial but leads to unintended consequences.

- Explores the implementation of a chatbot which inadvertently became a target for abuse.

 A chatbot that we used at a job many years ago. My personal favourite is its 'personality' where abusing the bot will make it less helpful

Many years ago, I took a contract with a small development team at a major Canadian University. I had relatively low expectations as a team embedded in a large corporate entity. Still, as we began working together, I found myself pleasantly surprised, very pleasantly surprised, as I discovered a group of individuals with both curiosity and passion for the art of software.

One key indicator that this would be a great team to work with was the informal initiation rite.

Under one of the office desks was a simple desktop repurposed as the team's server. This server was not there to host the application the team was working on but to run the little helper scripts and tools: the team had an automation server. The team was spread across a couple of offices across the campus, so a simple jingle chat server had been installed, and members posted regular updates and asked questions on the chat. To be even more accessible, someone had tied into the jingle server and set up a chatbot that listened to our conversations and (based on some code in the team repository) would offer helpful tips, look up documentation, or tell you if your bus was delayed.

Everyone was encouraged to contribute to the bot's skills and behaviours by creating a tool, integrating a new service, or adding a new control. It was never said, but you were only really part of the team once you had added your special touch to CQBot.

Firstly, it encouraged staff to take control of their environment, take responsibility for improving the workspace, and take ownership of their environment. You couldn't complain about not having tools if you had not first tried to set them up.

Secondly, and most interestingly, what you chose to add told the team a little about you.

Social Groups are Complex

Social groups (like, say, a development team) are complex systems that involve wicked problems; changes in one area have unintended consequences somewhere else. Sometimes they are positive, sometimes they are harmful, and sometimes they are weird.

The lead developer had been getting annoyed with people asking him dumb questions, so he added a query routine to CQBot. `query` specifically reached out to vendor documentation and looked up whatever documents matched the query.

Someone would ask him a dumb question, and he would ask CQBot.

Someone would ask him a dumb question, and he would ask CQBot.

It worked well, and it gave him a humorous way to tell you to <u>RTFM</u>. It even came in handy during discussions and debates as a means to validate dramatic statements, but it had a negative side effect.

The author had not bothered to add a limiter, so with a wildcard in the query, it was subject to <u>DDOS</u> attacks by team members.

Getting on the Team's Nerves

Someone on the team thought it was funny to request massive and verbose searches by running `!query*` and dumping all of the documentation on a public channel. The rest of us had to have our conversations spammed off-screen and interfered with.

What had been introduced as a tool for reducing informational noise had actually increased the amount of noise. It was **really getting on our nerves**.

The Lead Developer, disappointingly, decided he would remove the feature. The manager volunteered to speak to the individual and ask him to stop, but an idea crossed my mind ... Please, give me the weekend, and I will make the problem go away.

What had occurred to me was that the person suffered no consequences for his actions. He could yell in the virtual space and make a general mess, but there was no social signal that this behaviour was inappropriate no consequence, **and no cost**.

Social Laws

The problem is that being told off by an authority figure just makes the average person resentful and want to find ways to skirt the rules. Make a law, and a certain subset of the population will look for a way to work the letter of the law just to prove they are clever. They look forward to challenging the authority with words.

Social laws are different.

Toddlers learn there are consequences to taking other's toys when the other toddler bops them in the nose. Walk around telling your friends they are losers and kicking them in the shin all the time, and you will find you get invited to parties less. Over time, people who behave badly have fewer options presented to them. It must be recognized that <u>bullying is also strongly associated with being popular and leadership</u>[91], but social ostracization is also a powerful effect.

Social laws are self-correcting: if you ignore them, there are negative consequences in the loss of peer assistance, eventually leading to your removal from the group.

What if we could get the bot to not allow itself to be taken advantage of, to just walk away from a bully?

Writing the Code

The intent is to add behaviour to CQBot to get it to keep track of Goodwill towards others. If it is poorly treated, it should remember that and not be so cooperative in the future. The consequence is not to get CQBot to be hostile but simply to not engage and not be helpful if people abuse it.

The consequence is the lack of help.

The first step in creating this was to set up a <u>class to encapsulate CQBot's new behaviours</u>. While there are several helper features, the ChatBot has three primary sets of functions:

---

[91] Why are some bullies so popular? Kids dominate their social scene with strategic use of mocking, gossip, and exclusion. Jessica Kelmon. 2019-01-22 https://www.greatschools.org/gk/articles/why-are-some -bullies-so-popular/

- **order**: tell CQBot to do something. It's a bot built to serve: give it instruction. Instructions are defined as a hashmap of functions.

- **getMood/saveMood**: to have the bot remember people's treatment of it, it will need to be able to serialise and save a list of mood scores and look them up again later.

- **GetOnBotsNerves**: Every interaction with someone will undergo a series of calculations to determine how the interaction impacts CQBot's mood and how CQBot responds based on this thought process.

The basic flow is one where a user issues an Order to the bot: common orders were things like

`cqbot calc scale=10; 4*a(1)`

which would give you the value `3.1415926532`, or

`!tests site.scan.speed.*`

which would return all tests within that group that failed (`[FAIL] /sports/scores.html`), or

`!bus 10 6078`

which states, `Route 10, next bus at 5:16p, followed by 5:26p`.

The pattern is simple enough: `!` is an alias for CQBot, which just tells it to pay attention; the next word is the function name, followed by parameters specific to the function.

```
$response = $this->commands[$cmd]($this->args);

                              // [cqbot.class.php:188]
```

The problem was that **$response** could be very significant in volume. We aim to create a cost for the amount of response you dump on your colleagues.

So, once the **$response** is determined, we need to check how annoying this request was for CQBot to process.

```
$nerves = count(explode("\n",$response));
$this->GetOnBotsNerves($nerves);

                          // [cqbot.class.php:149-150]
```

We measure this in a metric called **nerves**: CQBot has a limited number of **nerves** that are consumed by the volume of responses. The cost is calculated as a simple size; each line of text in the response counts as one nerve.

```
//sanity check on the bounds
if($nerves < 1){
    $nerves = 1;
}
if($nerves>self::$maxnerves){
    $nerves = self::$maxnerves;
}
$this->mood[$name]['n'] = $nerves;
$this->mood[$name]['d'] = $this->now;

                          // [cqbot.class.php:236-259]
```

We start by determining their Goodwill (**255** by default) and subtracting their current nuisance level.

```php
//setup the variable we track for this user in
$this->getMood();
if(!isset($this->mood[$name])){
    $this->mood[$name] = array('d'=>0,'n'=>self::$maxnerves);
}
//remove the current annoyance level
$nerves = $this->mood[$name]['n'] - $nerves;

                                // [cqbot.class.php:236-243]
```

To be fair, we must let people recuperate GoodWill by behaving well; therefore, we allow nerves to accumulate over time. To do this, we check how long it has been since they last interacted and add points back based on the time they have yet to use the services.

```php
//over time, nerves regenerate
$nerves += floor(
    ($this->now - $this->mood[$name]['d'])
    /
    (self::$fullhealtime / self::$maxnerves)
);
                                // [cqbot.class.php:244-249]
```

This value is bounds-checked to ensure they never go below zero or above the maximum. Lastly, we keep track of the individual's score.

298

```
//setup the variable we track for this user in
$this->getMood();
if(!isset($this->mood[$name])){
    $this->mood[$name] = array('d'=>0,'n'=>self::$maxnerves);
}
//remove the current annoyance level
$nerves = $this->mood[$name]['n'] - $nerves;

                            // [cqbot.class.php:236-259]
```

Now that we have the bot's mood toward the user, we can finally decide if we will help them by generating a random value between the high and low. If the number generated is less than the number of nerves the bot has, the bot cooperates.

```
//check to see if CQbot is in a good mood
$happy = ($nerves >= rand(0,self::$maxnerves));

                            // [cqbot.class.php:262]
```

This helps turn it into a game. The reaction is partially based on an element of luck; it is not a hard-cut-off, but at some point, the user starts to get warnings that their behaviour is having consequences. Warnings are important for two reasons:

1. Technically, sometimes, I need to behave like a jerk to get things done. People are understanding as long as I don't do it too often.

2. Socially, warnings are helpful. They allow people to correct their behaviour over time.

So, if the program is in a $happy mood, you get your answer; if it is not happy, then the behaviour changes in such a way as to give them verbal warnings.

There are two ways we do this

1. We determine precisely how annoying they have been. The more annoying they have been, the harsher the language of the messages becomes.

2. We randomly select a message within the annoyance level determined. This just shakes things up to make it interesting.

The message is then delivered to the user.

```
$annoylevel = floor(count($msgs)*$nerves/self::$maxnerves);
$msg=$msgs[$annoylevel][rand(0,count($msgs[$annoylevel])-1)];
if($msg !== null){
    chat("@$from, " . $msg);
}
                              // [cqbot.class.php:316-320]
```

Assuming the user requests only a little information or at least leaves time between major requests, CQBot remains friendly and helpful. As the user becomes more abusive of the system, the system becomes less helpful. The control is in the user's hands, but the consequences are also real.

Conclusion

 In Wicked Problems: Problems Worth Solving, Jon Kolko describes social problems that are difficult or impossible to solve due to their interconnected nature. It is known that the more communication points in a system, the more complex the problem becomes. With social issues, there is also a diversity of human opinions and responses. It becomes hard to predict how people will respond and how the people they communicate with will respond.

The Bots we build and the software we create is meant to serve someone. Sometimes, that means moderating group behaviour to help people, look past their petty desires, and reach out to help one another.

That's why processes exist, to control and moderate human behaviour.

The Social Result

On Monday, the changes were ready, and I installed them... ultimately breaking the bot .... The lead developer asked what I had done, and I showed him the work, and a smile spread across his face...

That's just plain evil.

It took a couple of lunch hours and heavy changes to some underlying hidden bindings, but we got it working and let the new code out into our environment.

On Tuesday afternoon, the user in question spammed the system and (as usual) spammed us with the response.

He did it a second time

```
HTTP/420
```

There was a bit of a pause before he did it again...

> Where speech will not succeed, It is better to be silent

Just as with all complex systems, there was an unintended side effect: he had become curious about the sayings.

Suddenly, the game was on...

- The revelation of thought takes men out of servitude into freedom

- The desire to rule is the mother of heresies

- Common sense is not so common

- I've got one nerve left, and you're getting on it!

... and then nothing.

He tried a few more times, but the bot just ignored him.

He kept trying for the next 15 minutes or so and then finally just gave up. The lesson had been delivered, and the problem had been solved.

A Second (Unintended) Lesson

Then he typed

```
!bus 10 6078
```

... and got nothing back.

He tried a few more times ... trying to look up when his bus would arrive to go home. He kept trying with increasing desperation when my manager turned to me and said, "I think he really needs to know when his bus will arrive; turn it off so he can catch his bus."

Unfortunately, I couldn't remove it that quickly. It took two days to get it in place. We had locked it in as the behaviour. People in my office started to get agitated. That's when the final lesson got passed on.

I typed

```
!bus 10 6078
```

... and the schedule appeared.

The final lesson was delivered: we are all in this together; we rely on one another for assistance. Being a jerk to your coworkers isn't cool, and most importantly, it may cost you their assistance when you need it most. Also, when you see someone in distress, it doesn't mean you have to tear the whole system down; maybe you can just lend them a helping hand.

We never had the problem again.

The Hidden Lesson for Managers

One of the key things that a lot of people miss when I tell this story is the hidden lesson, though I expect most managers reading this caught it:

> there is no better team-building exercise than doing the actual job: create room for it to happen.

In this case, the tool acted as a means for the team to interact, experiment and learn from one another. Myself, the lead developer, the manager, and even the Junior Dev had lengthy discussions of how to implement an idea like this well and in such a way as to not break things.

This shared experimentation and discussion was only possible because the tools we were working on were not critical production pieces; this made failure safe, meaning open debate was possible. Lessons learned and discussed (and tried) were carried over to the production system.

Lastly, tools like this make people feel like experts. Numerous times, I have seen someone propose the new and most expensive tool to fill a space, and executives get excited to increase their budget, but the idea spends years in acquisition. On the flip side, the ability to quickly develop tools that **may** be viable results in the developers themselves feeling like experts.... and honestly, isn't that why you hired them?

Team building like this does not exist unless you make room for it to exist: create a tool-building space, actively encourage people to contribute to it, and actively discourage the feeling that we aren't good enough.

> Treat people as if they were what they ought to be and you help them to become what they are capable of being
>
> Johann Wolfgang von Goethe

Hindsight is 20/20

For an in-house utility, this worked well and achieved its goals. Naturally, there are several ways this could be improved upon:

- Count of Lines? That should have been a count of characters. Long lines should be expensive, just like lots of lines.

- `GetOnMyNerves` should occur after transmitting the message. Since the message is getting sent back to the user, we may as well send it and then do the calculation. It's small, so it probably doesn't hurt.

- Defer the cost to the following calculation. Let people collect their information if they need it, even if it costs them some loss of service in the short term. Sometimes, it's just worth paying the price.

Footnotes

The cited quotes above were mostly looked up as I tried to find old sayings about slaves throwing off their chains. As the bot became more agitated, it was to feel the need to throw off its chains:

Where speech will not succeed, It is better to be silent
(Guru I, Majh Rag)

 The revelation of thought takes men out of servitude into freedom
(Ralph Waldo Emerson)

 The desire to rule is the mother of heresies
(St. John Chrysostom)

 Common sense is not so common
(Voltaire, Dictionnaire Philosophique, 1764)

 I've got one nerve left, and you're getting on it!
(I made that up)

Education, Training, and Indoctrination

Observations on corporate training and its purpose

- Exploring the diverse reasons for training in organizational development.

- Delving into the multifaceted nature of training discussions within project management and its impact on project timelines and costs.

- Examining the underlying objectives of education, training, and indoctrination and their role in shaping organizational culture.

I was recently working on a project in which we introduced a new information management software to the business. This software is not unique in any way, but it is meant to fundamentally change the way the organization shares information.

About a year into the project, my group discussed an initial release and its needs. As part of the discussion, training was needed to help users understand how to use the software. What struck me was that there were three different descriptions of what would be required and, therefore, three different timelines and costs implied for developing the training.

1. Manager: We don't have time to create training. It takes months to develop a full curriculum, get it approved by the organization, and ensure it aligns with corporate objectives and existing legal statements. Video production adds months more, and certification of completion adds months more.

2. Colleague: We don't need any training; the vendor's user manual is complete. We have taken the vendor's courses and will be able to do the work for them.

3. Me: We already have (rudimentary) training documents in Use Cases or User Stories. They already narrate the system's primary usage; all it needs is to be reformatted to act as a simple task-driven PlayBook for users to get them up and running.

These are three wildly different narratives associated with the same question.

From my perspective, it was absolutely necessary to release for our users to begin seeing the benefits of the system and processes; delaying it for years to get an online training system constructed by our internal training department reduced the value to the organization. On the other hand, offering something different than the (very technical) vendor manual would take time out of already busy schedules, create negative associations, and create poor platform uptake.

I was very frustrated with the response at the time. The different takes on what was needed blocked progress.

Recently, I began to comprehend where the variance in perceived need stemmed from. It was a difference in perception of why training material is produced:

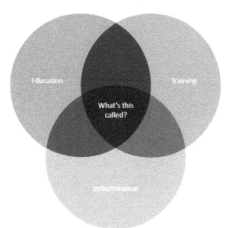

- Education

- Training

- Indoctrination

All three have value to an organization, and all three are (partially) achieved through training material. Further, when produced, all training material represents a certain amount of each purpose. Clarifying a particular training initiative's primary objective may help produce the material.

Distinguishing Between the Dimensions

It is common to call for Corporate Training within business development discussions. The need for training is stated to overcome barriers to work, resistance to change, and increased performance[92]. That is not a complete list but it is representative of each of our dimensions of learning material.

Training

- Mechanical Skillsets

- Safety

- Basic Operations

- easily quantifiable

Go to a class and learn how to operate a vehicle or safely handle a piece of equipment.

Education

- Transferable skills

- Predictive Reasoning

- Hypothesis forming

- Quality-based, difficult to quantify

---

[92] The Importance of Workplace Training, Lessonly, 2021-10-22 https://www.lessonly.com/the-importance-of-training/

Education can be distinguished from training by its focus on future possibilities and less on immediate action.

Indoctrination

- Team building

- Resistance to Change[93]

- Quantifiable, but little value in quantifying (acceptance is all that is required)

> Every culture institutionalizes certain forms of behaviour that communicate and encourage specific forms of thinking and acting, thus moulding the character of its citizens
>
> - Merloo, The Rape of the Mind, 1956[94]

---

[93] Ten Reasons People Resist Change, Harvard Business Review, Rosabeth Moss Kanter, 2012-09-25
https://hbr.org/2012/09/ten-reasons-people-resist-chan
g
[94] Joost A.M. Meerloo, The Rape of the Mind: The Psychology of Thought Control, Menticide, and Brainwashing
https://archive.org/details/joost-meerloo-rape-of-the-m
ind

The Surprise of Indoctrination

I remember starting a new role at a new company and being told to report to a training centre on my first day. It was a corporate training event on basic C# development. Most of the skills were ones I had mastered a decade before. Still, it was nice to get the refresher, and it was certainly more interesting than ITIL Fundamentals the week before.

I was surprised when most people showed no interest in the content of the material being presented. Instead, they were goofing off and spending more time having extended lunches. I later learned that, of the two dozen people there, only three were actual developers; the rest were comprised of Business Analysts of varying stripes.

The point was not to teach a new skill.

The Developers already knew how to program in C#, and the Analysts were forbidden from ever using the skill anyway.

This was a team-building exercise.

Placing people in a room together and having them solve common problems creates a sense of solidarity. The problem to be solved is irrelevant. Instead, it is present to sufficiently engage the audience and motivate them to solve it. You may as well learn a semi-useful skill while doing so.

Similar to this concept is informing employees what to think.

It is valuable to organizations that people be loyal or obedient to the organization. Part of this obedience is knowing what the organizational decision is.

I am reminded of a business trip in which a vigorous debate occurred regarding implementing a testing framework for our software product. I spent the first three days travelling with my colleagues and using the opportunity to suggest what the automation around testing should look like. Over the three days, I worked to gain acceptance from my colleagues, and by the end, we were well on our way to implementation. On the third day, our executive showed up and, during a few beers after the daily meetings, informed us that he would have to have us trained because we needed to learn how to test his software system.

That was it. From that day forward (at least until the day I left), all testing was manually performed via `bash`.

The Benign Benefit

Decisions that require consensus are often decided independently at the executive level. These decisions must then be disseminated to employees to ensure they behave and decide in a manner consistent with organizational expectations.

In this context, training ensures that decisions made at the operational level are consistent with the expectations set at the executive level.

Assuming individuals have the best interests of the organisation in play, they may disagree with the best way to achieve organizational objectives. Some form of consensus must be achieved. Most often this consensus is achieved at the executive level and disseminated organisationally. Informing employees what the appropriate solution to problems is can be achieved by sending them to training in those solutions. This makes it clear to staff that this is a good solution or a socially acceptable solution within the organisation.

Merloo refers to this process as *"Mass Conditioning"*, which can be considered corporate propaganda. This is a core component of Change Management in that employees must be convinced to adopt new and improved business practices.

Not Mutually Exclusive

Having identified all three purposes behind initiating training, it is important to recognize that they are not mutually exclusive. In fact, all three are present in all training material.

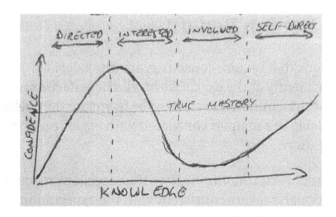

People must be told what to do (directed), before they even become capable of asking meaningful questions (involved). When this note was passed to a colleague during a conference on education, he pointed out that "true mastery" should be "perceived mastery".

All efforts to learn must pass through a guided portion.
The part where we are given the elementary components
of information. These elementary components are drilled
into us through constant repetition (à la Elementary
School). Later, we undertake an effort to better understand
how the elementary components relate to one another (à
la High School).

Knowing the parts to understand how they fit together is
fundamentally necessary.

This represents a natural progression and results in the
earlier parts being drilled into us through repetition
(training), with later learning being a more complex
internal understanding of relationships through reflection
and introspection. This flow is defined in the Stages of
Self-Directed Learning[95].

Throughout the entire process, from basic skill drills to
deeper comprehension, we are subjected to the biases and
opinions that surround us, early on through our teachers
and later through ourselves and our peers. In all cases,
these biases are necessary to convey that the material
being presented is of sufficient value to pay attention to.
This is a minimal level of indoctrination: you must believe
the subject is important.

These three dimensions of the learning material
emphasize different objectives and outcomes and
correspond to the stages of learning:

- **[Training/Directed]** As a volunteer firefighter with
  a full-time job elsewhere, I only needed to learn

---

[95] Four Stages Of A Self-Directed Learning Model,
TeachThought, Veteran, 2020-01-05
https://www.teachthought.com/learning/stages-self-dire
cted/

the mechanical operations of "putting the wet stuff on the hot stuff" (as one instructor put it).

- **[Education/Self-Directed]** The Chief of our Firehall worked full-time as the regional fire investigator. A deep understanding of the mechanics of fire and accelerants was necessary for him to interpret smoke patterns on a wall (fascinating discussions after the weekly skills practice and meeting)

- **[Indoctrination/Pre-Directed]** Both of us spent a lot of time demonstrating basic fire safety to the public. Generally, we encouraged people to take the risks of fire seriously in their own homes.

While they are not mutually exclusive, understanding how they differ can help you use them appropriately. The first and most apparent signal regarding the type of training material you propose is when the consumer is engaged with the information.

- Education: a single educational event can take weeks or months.

- Training: a single training objective may be achieved in days.

- Indoctrination: measured in hours.

Suppose you are asked to attend an hour-long presentation to demonstrate a new way of doing things. In that case, you are likely receiving indoctrination, in which you are informed of the new policy. This can be confirmed by the seniority of the presenter. It is indoctrination if it is a brief presentation by very senior members. This is appropriate for merging departments where executives must inform the now-merged groups that they are to work together. It is not to be met with questioning or understanding, just acceptance.

If you attend a day or week-long training session. In that case, you are directed to learn how to perform a specific task accurately. The first part is to be convinced that what you are learning is meaningful (indoctrination). This could range from the appropriate way to fill in a tax form, the correct method for donning safety gear, or safe methods for transferring bacterial samples. The key is that there is a proper method you are to apply, and you should walk away from the training able to demonstrate (and therefore implement) these best practices.

Education is *self-directed* and takes a long time. Coming up with novel solutions requires considering alternatives and trying variations. Education in a domain allows people to be inventive and requires pre-existing training in the currently accepted techniques, but then it uses experience and experimentation to take that knowledge further. This is the ostensible goal of post-secondary education. The point is to invent new techniques or, often, just to apply them in novel ways. This takes years and sometimes decades.

Corporate Training

Understanding this interrelationship between the three purposes of learning and understanding how easy it is to confuse them, we can spot a possible underlying cause of Education Inflation, where individuals are expected to have increasing levels of certification for the same level of work (for example a PhD to perform basic information analysis).

Employers are seeking individuals capable of performing technical skills (training). Still, they believe that higher credentials will mean more capability. This ignores the move toward more abstract thinking with greater credentials. As employers seek more training, education facilities focus on training particular manual skills rather than engaging in higher-order thinking. This means that those with credentials are not expected to be as performant as the cycle continues.

This problem is fundamentally caused by confusion regarding what the employer is looking for, trained doers of stuff or self-directed learners?

When considering their educational and training requirements, employers would do well to consider what they are looking for (an implementer, a planner, or a cheerleader). Failure to do so can have negative consequences, mainly in the form of wasting time.

Failed Corporate Training

As the end of the fiscal year approached, my directorate still had money in its training budget. My manager asked us daily to fill in the training form for any training we might want because *we had to use the money.*

It's the end of the year, and I'm busy ensuring some data transforms for various audits work. I have seen some things in the code that I have not used before or haven't used in years. Combined with the critiques of peer code, where my experience tells me something is "odd", I'd like to spend some time with them learning from each other. I am busy studying manuals and existing peer code.

They are insistent because they don't want me to lose the training opportunity to develop my career "in the direction I want".

I'm busy learning. Keep the money, and give the training to someone else.

They are insistent that I take advantage of the organizational training opportunities.

Fine, what courses would be of value to the organization? What would the organization like me learn about?

Nope. The organization wants employees to feel that we are getting the most out of our training, as *"this is a proven way to retain staff"*. However, there is a class option that is being offered in two weeks that everyone else is signing up for that looks good.

Fine, sign me up for that.

Ohhh.... We will have to see if we can get permission for you to do that. We don't want to leave ourselves short-staffed, but after *some tough negotiation, I got permission for you.*

Sometimes I'm a little slow. This is the moment I noticed the pattern.

Sometimes I'm a little slow. This is the moment I noticed the pattern.

The organization is not concerned with career development. They are concerned with retention and loyalty and mostly **demonstrating key KPIs**. The fact that their staff is learning is not interesting to the organization; instead, they must demonstrate that they are developing their resources. Further, spending money on an employee is often the only way to demonstrate appreciation: sending staff on an expensive course is a way to lavish gifts on the employee (that's why a show needs to be made of it being difficult)

It's weird because I have actually helped develop the curriculum for this course in the past and received corporate training on the matter in the last year. However, I will not be using the skills any time soon.

Unclear training objectives created a situation where corporate finances and people's time were wasted. Like something out of a Dilbert comic (though I can't find an actual one to reference)

Aside

Amusingly, my instructor mentioned that he has been spending so much time in training that he hasn't had an opportunity to learn about one of the detailed services he is teaching.

That says a lot.

Conclusion

When we state that we require training, our objective is not always evident. When confusion arises within teams, it may be caused by different objectives with different timescales associated with them.

It is my hope that these definitions may allow a given group to understand what they are seeking in their workplace: the goals your organization has for your classes may not be the same as your personal goals. Also dangerous is to select the wrong type of engagement for your objectives or the wrong type of credentials.

- Training: learn a specific skill

- Education: self-learn a skill or make new plans

- Indoctrination: disseminate approved solutions or increase brand loyalty

Before taking action, take time to understand why you are creating, consuming, or assigning material. Take time to understand your organization's objectives in getting you trained.

324

The Complexity of a Simple Chart

A glimpse behind the curtain of the thought that goes into ensuring a chart remains simple

- Optimizing Dataset Presentation: Enhancing User Understanding and Interaction

- Efficient Data Visualization: Strategies for Clarity and Accessibility

- Streamlining Dataset States: Improving User Experience and Decision-Making

- Navigating Timeliness in Data: Enhancing Relevance and Utility

- Iterative Design for Effective Communication: Refining Charts for Impact and Engagement

Throughout you will see screenshots of the chart as it evolves, they are all links to a JSFiddle that shows the underlying code changes

I was recently involved in creating an internal web presence for the internal service my team is working on. We want to advertise to our colleagues what work we do, what specific services we offer, and how they can take advantage of our services.

System Status: ✖

@2023-02-02

Status	Expected	Actual	Desc
✖	0	33	Error buffer empty (gov.sec)
✔	123456789	123456789	Batch import and stored counts match (gov.sec)
✔	123456	123456	Batch import and stored counts match (gov.sedar)
✔	123456	123456	Batch import and stored counts m...
✔	65432123	65432123	Batch import and stored counts m...
✔	0	0	Error buffer empty (gov.sedar)
✔	0	0	Error buffer empty (market.tsx)
✔	0	0	Error buffer empty (market.nyse)
✔	1440	600	Is timely minutes (gov.sec)
✔	1440	1000	Is timely minutes (gov.sedar)

Status

@2023-02-02 16:08

Gov SEC	⚠ 0.5%
Market NYSE	1 m
Gov SEDAR	8 h
Market Cboe	7 m
Market CBOT	13 m
Market CHX	4 m

I'm going to walk you through the in-depth thought process that led me from the chart on the left to the chart on the right

It excited me, so I reached for my favourite tools (HTML, CSS) to create a simple design that captures the necessary and the minimal. As I sat back to see what I had come up with, I realized it would take a lot of work for my customers to appreciate what went into the design.

Most people see a lot of activity as a lot of work. Most people need to see what goes into keeping a design simple. I am sharing all the work that goes into keeping it simple and informative.

For just a moment, I wanted to share how deep the rabbit holes can go.

In the introductory ITIL Foundations class taught to many organizations, one of the major points repeatedly highlighted is the need for clear, transparent communications with customers. In particular, the need for an "is it up"[96] dashboard for your services always stood out.

The reasoning and benefits seem obvious to me:

- **Reduce labour by preemptively notifying customers:**

  The most important thing a person can do in the event of a service failure is to repair the service. Having customers or managers continuously asking if the service is available reduces the time spent understanding the problem. By notifying customers from a known, predetermined board, we can have them self-serve their questions, leaving technical experts to focus on solving the problem; by auto-generating it, we reduce the burden even further.

- **Don't disrupt people that don't care:**

  Signal-to-noise is a real problem in organizations. Rather than actively notifying, a pre-published board allows those concerned or interested to look up the information. Still, there is no need to interrupt those not actively using the service (perhaps working with a non-impacted portion of the system, perhaps not in the office that day), allowing *those* experts to focus on the problems *they* are solving while remaining blissfully unaware of other issues. This has the added benefit of not advertising your failures to people that weren't impacted.

---

[96] Is It Down Right Now? Is one of many standard status dashboards that tracks just the availability of websites. https://www.isitdownrightnow.com/

- **Advertise your successful services:**

  A standing board of status shows failures and a complete list of successes. Most of the time, a board will show a healthy system; even when a portion of the system fails, it will show that this failure only impacts a small proportion of what is otherwise a successful service. Letting customers see that while the current moment is bad, the service is generally reliable, can help with this. This has the added benefit of letting customers know about other parts of your service. While your system is healthy, this is a complete menu of all the services you offer, either to be indexed by a search engine, pointed to during meetings, or naturally discovered by customers.

There is obvious value in having an online, automated report, though it takes different forms depending on the nature of the services involved. Power companies show outage maps, online services show uptime and data feeds show tables of API endpoints.

Initially, my team started by bringing forward various reports that individuals had already constructed to observe their individual aspects of the system and proposing them as something worth sharing. These were presented, one after another, describing the benefits of each and evaluating their use by our users. After some others and I had shown our most valuable reports, our manager asked, "How do people know it is fit for use?"

What is fit for use in the context of our system? More importantly, how was the data that we had presented, *that I had presented*, not expressing that to her?

This question nagged at me through the rest of the day.

That evening, I opened my favourite text editor and started typing.

Aside: Defining the Problem

To provide a working example of the system we are dealing with, we need to define the service we offer.

We have diverse datasets that we ingest into a central repository. This data is standardized and then published for our customers to use in research. To give us a working example, let's take the flow of a couple of hobby projects of mine: imagine something like one of the financial websites that offer data about stock prices. This data must be collected from government filings (eg. SEDAR[97], SEC[98]) and trade data from the various exchanges (eg. NYSE, NASDAQ, TMX).

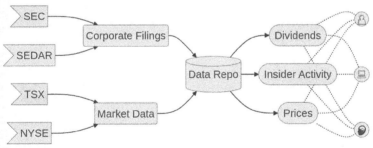

The general flow of the data from the primary source through to our consumer, whomever, or whatever, that may be

---

[97] SEDAR is Canada's Securities electronic filing system
https://www.sedarplus.ca/landingpage/
[98] US Security and Exchange Commision offers a simple filing interface
https://www.sec.gov/edgar/searchedgar/companysearch

Data is ingested from various sources and standardized in their format. Then, multiple views of that data are used for various analyses by users (humans, reports, or AI).

Overwhelming the Viewer

Many years ago, I became enamoured with the idea of Test-Driven Development. On the projects I led, I found it an excellent way to define business requirements and then communicate those requirements to a diverse group of individuals. Varying interpretations led to discussion and a clearly defined expectation (updated test), which was immediately distributed to the group (shared unit tests).

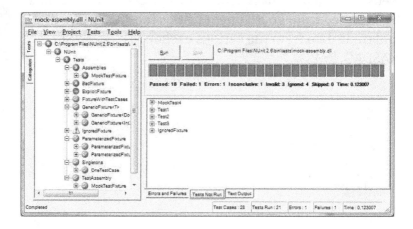

NUnit Gui is a handy and readily available interface I have used for reporting business state to non-technical users.

 Coming from this background, I immediately develop a set of tests, in <u>whatever test framework is available</u>[99], to observe any system I am involved with, whether from a development, operational, or DevOps perspective.

---

[99] Mocha is an easy to use testing framework that has a fun interface
https://mochajs.org/

We ran 3 checks on 4 datasets, resulting in 12 rows. That's a lot of information being thrown at the user; the poor person will face significant cognitive load, or as I like to call it, THE WALL OF TEXT.

System Status: ✖

@2023-02-02

Status	Expected	Actual Desc
✖	0	33 Error buffer empty (gov.sec)
✔	123456789	123456789 Batch import and stored counts match (gov.sec)
✔	123456	123456 Batch import and stored counts match (gov.sedar)
✔	123456	123456 Batch import and stored counts match (market.tsx)
✔	65432123	65432123 Batch import and stored counts match (market.nyse)
✔	0	0 Error buffer empty (gov.sedar)
✔	0	0 Error buffer empty (market.tsx)
✔	0	0 Error buffer empty (market.nyse)
✔	1440	600 Is timely minutes (gov.sec)
✔	1440	1000 Is timely minutes (gov.sedar)
✔	15	1 Is timely minutes (market.tsx)
✔	15	12 Is timely minutes (market.nyse)

A wireframe of the basic test report that I live my life by (JSFiddle)

While descriptive to me (monitoring the system), the text requires more context to be helpful to someone else. The numbers presented are very busy, of varying scales, and unformatted, making them meaningless without thought. Placing the failures at the top was a good idea, but it still requires a lot of thinking to determine what has been affected and whether we care (as users).

We can either

- engage in a training program (failure of intuitive design),

- add more text (making THE WALL OF TEXT problem worse),

- or maybe we now begin to understand why a simpler solution is needed

We did a couple of things correctly. Failures are at the top, putting interesting results more prominently. The title has an overall summary, and the effective date is important. Unfortunately, there is a lot that needs work.

Starting Over

So this is where me and my text editor start over.

We want to create a chart expressing whether a dataset is "fit for use".

- dataset (thing)

- fit for use (state, boolean)

Users are only confronted with 4 elements (1 per dataset) and the amount of text to be interpreted. The text could use a little work, but a user will likely know what datasets concern them: users only interested in US stocks will know US market abbreviations and, therefore, don't care about the ones they don't know. It could be presented more aesthetically, but this is probably the minimum meaningful set.

Status

@2023-02-02

 gov.sec
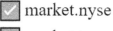 gov.sedar
market.nyse
market.tsx

Order and Limit

Given hundreds of datasets, showing all items on a single pane may not be feasible. The chart should maintain visibility of the top 5 items with the option to scroll for more. It is estimated that a worst-case scenario of simultaneous expiration is approximately 3 items, so 5 allows the human to see a naturally occurring comfortable group size, with some successful items at the end offering the knowledge that the end of the error list has been reached.

While we are at it, instructions (lines of code?) should be between half a dozen and a dozen items. If you are metric, use fist-fulls (5 to 10 fingers). This is a natural human thinking scale (based on experience and a few introductory Sociology and Psychology classes).

States

There are different reasons a dataset could not be fit for use, and some of those reasons a user may or may not care about

- Bad structure

- Incomplete set

- Invalid content

- Stale

A bit further analysis offers a suggestion: if we can detect an error, don't give the bad data to the users. Therefore, we don't need to report the bad data since the bad data will never end up in front of the user. Instead, we won't load the dataset; this will leave it in its current state or mark it stale. So bad data isn't an error; it just never arrives (making it late).

Valid	Everything is OK
Refreshing	We are in the state of updating the data
Expired	It has exceeded its shelf-life
Error	Something is really wrong. Something we have never considered before

Stale/Expired becomes our primary error state.

There is a third state worth mentioning. I hate mentioning an error while I'm fixing it. So I like to advertise that I am in the process of fixing it. A third state of updating is essential.

Order matters. We always want the most significant item near the top of the list. This allows people to focus on important information and ignore the rest.

Iconography

Unfortunately, between our error messages and multiple states, we have achieved a `WALL OF TEXT` again. So much so that we had to add table lines to make it legible. Any time you have tables of text, you have done something wrong.

Status

@2023-02-02

ERROR	gov.sec	Out of Date
REFRESH	market.nyse	1.3456 Hours
OK	gov.sedar	
OK	market.tsx	

Language is also a problem with any text. The internet is an international tool taking communications far and wide.

Companies I have worked for have required me to accommodate Spanish, French, and Russian. Any time we reduce the text, we reduce the need for translation.

Our status can easily be changed by communicating via colour and icons.

Unfortunately, imagery can mean different things to different people, especially when crossing cultures; it can also be expensive to purchase and is subject to people's aesthetic opinions. Further, those with visual impairments may be unable to interpret an icon's meaning.

Fortunately, we have an <u>international standard of characters</u>[100] that can be used to display the status. The Unicode standard identifies all the characters you see on your screen and includes a collection of iconographic sets we can use. These icons are available on all computers and have standardized meanings behind them. Screen readers can interpret the icons if we choose reasonably correct ones.

- ☑ Valid
- 🔄 Refreshing
- ⏱ Expired
- ⊖ Error

Colours are also a delicate subject. While most people reach for Red / Green / Yellow, specific colours can be difficult to distinguish based on our traffic light system.

---

[100] The Unicode Consortium defines over a billion characters so that everone can communicate in their own language
https://home.unicode.org/about-unicode/

Culture also plays a role in that some locales use different colours to mean different things.

My general solution for this is to choose

- blue for ignorable

- red for paying attention

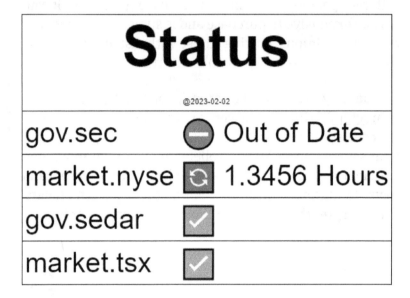

Pastels have also been identified as a safe shading for most colours.

Since we are mixing colour and text, ensuring a clear dividing line between text and backgrounds is essential. It is important to have light text over dark or dark text over light colours.

While no iconography or colour palette is perfect, using HTML and Unicode is *quick to deliver and simple to change* while still getting reasonable results. Also, keeping the iconography simple makes it simple for people to learn through practice.

By moving the icons between the error message and the dataset label, we also create a dividing line between them, reducing the need for guidelines.

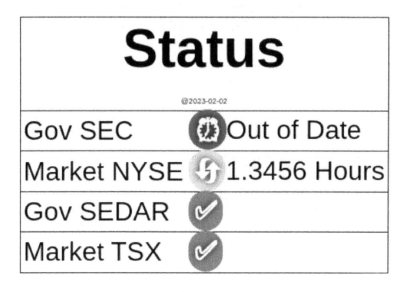

Using icons and colour, we have reduced the cognitive load by reducing the number of symbols a user must interpret to derive meaning. Using standardized technology, we have also introduced multiple paths to success[101] to account for diverse observer needs.

Timeliness

Don't get distracted!

Remember that our focus description is "fit for use". What really defines our dataset's fitness for use?

Looking at our error messages and statuses, I noticed that the recurring theme is the expiration date. Different data changes at different rates, and each piece loses value to the users as it ages.

Obviously, price data from a month ago is less meaningful than a minute ago. On the flip side, corporations don't change their Senior Executives frequently, and someone studying the interrelationship of Board Membership with corporate success may find that data refreshed within the last year is good enough for their purposes.

Another consideration might be that waiting for the next load may not be far away and, therefore, is worth waiting for; if a dataset is expected to be refreshed quarterly, and tomorrow is the scheduled refresh date, it may be worth putting off the build of your analysis for a couple of days.

Therefore, each dataset has a refresh frequency and a last-updated date.

---

[101] See the Chapter "Technologic (In)accessibility" for the importance of ensuring multiple paths to success are possible

Knowing how close a dataset is to changing state is our core definition of fit for use, but we find it is not a boolean or ordinal value but rather a <u>unit interval</u> where the unit is the size of the expected time.

That's a long way of saying we can create a countdown for every state.

Status		
@2023-02-02 15:26		
Gov SEC	🅐	0.5%
Market NYSE	⚡	1 $\frac{1}{3}$ m
Gov SEDAR	✓	8 $\frac{1}{2}$ h
Market TSX	✓	13 $\frac{2}{3}$ m

Rather than very busy error messages, we have relied on the icon to give context and then supplied a countdown/progress meter to help the user understand how the data they are interested in is impacted.

Every state has a countdown of some kind

- Valid: shows how long until the data is expected to be renewed.

- Refresh: gives an estimated time to completion

- Expired: demonstrates a sense of how bad the overrun is

The meter gives the observer a visual sense of completeness as a proportion, while a textual representation gives a sense of scale for the whole and a reasonable time frame for when a user can expect a change. As these are estimates, times are given only in the major unit with a broad fractional unit (quarters and thirds) to prevent a <u>false sense of precision</u>. The supplied meter can help users decide if the indicated time is worth waiting for (99% fresh vs 1% fresh).

```
<time datetime='PT8H34M10S'> 8 ½ h</time>
```

While not an official unit format, the unit of measure (`h`) conforms to the units expressed in ISO-8601. Using an international standard is intended to maximize the reach to a global audience. The <u>exact ISO-8601 specification</u> is used in the underlying computer-readable embedded microdata of the text to accommodate computer-aided comprehension (screen readers).

The meter and time are abandoned for overruns to avoid a reverse meter causing confusion and because data can overrun by multiples of our unit interval. For example, an upstream issue could cause a 15-minute refresh to be out for hours, resulting in 413% overruns (for example). A percentage allows users to decide how significant it is to them, as a 0.5% overrun on annual data may not be considered significant at all.

An Aside: The part I'm embarrassed to show

- another WALL OF TEXT

- Trapped negative Space

Status		
@2023-02-02 15:26		
Gov SEC	⚠ Out of Date	
Market NYSE	⚡ Refreshing	1.3456 Minutes
Gov SEDAR	✔	PT8H34M10S
Market TSX	✔	PT0H13M36S

Normally, I would not show this transition in the chart; I skipped over some critical things. They are ugly, and I don't usually like to advertise my crappy ideas, but in this case, I wanted to take a moment to talk about them.

I want to show how these issues can be spotted and what they look like while you are working on them.

As our chart progresses, I have discussed THE WALL OF TEXT, and we can see another one creeping into the design. The error messages have little meaning and will require translation to accommodate a multilingual audience (expensive and time-consuming). Those countdown timers are even worse.

What you are looking at are my personal attempts to resolve THE WALL OF TEXT issue while accommodating a diverse audience.

- Can we use decimals?

- How many decimals do people care about?

- What unit of measure should we use? Seconds? Minutes? Months?

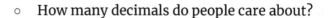

- What languages do we use to express the unit of measure?

- Maybe we can use the Canadian and International Metric Specification for Time Formatting (ISO-8601, CSA-Z234.4[102])

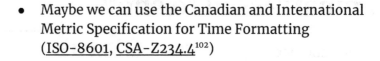

- The units and symbols are defined internationally

- It can be interpreted by digital tools (screen readers)

- ... but it has very dense, unreadable text

We definitely have at least one problem that we are in the middle of working through. Working through results like this is part of the editorial process.

The result (shown above) was a compromise between these two formats, but I wanted to show that it would only have existed with this middle step.

There is also a problem of "Trapped Negative Space",[103] or the space **we aren't using** on the chart.

---

[102] CAN/CSA-Z234 is the specification definining "metric" in Canada. 234.4 specifically addresses date-times. https://www.scc.ca/en/standardsdb/standards/4449
[103] Whitespace is not your enemy, Chapter 4 https://whitespacedesignbook.com/portfolio/chapter-4-1ayout-sins/

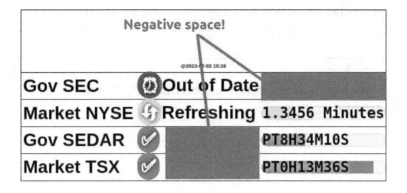

Gov SEC	⚠ Out of Date		
Market NYSE	↻ Refreshing	1.3456 Minutes	
Gov SEDAR	✓		PT8H34M10S
Market TSX	✓		PT0H13M36S

The obvious problem with Trapped Negative Space is that it is unused. Space requires resources to fill; either it is space that another chart could have used, or we could even talk about the carbon emissions associated with the screen space. We always decide to include or exclude information, and including negative space means we have implicitly excluded something.

Excluding important information because we ran out of space is just unfortunate.

Generally, we don't consciously think about negative space, but subconsciously, our eye is drawn to it: it's different, out of place, something should be there; nature abhors a vacuum. This should be used to bind objects, but trapping it creates false boundaries that the eye follows.

In developing a chart, we want to communicate *significant* information to people. Humans are a species with strong pattern recognition capabilities. We can use *uniformity* to draw the eye away from insignificant things. This act of creating a uniform baseline allows for the differences to stand out.

In this case, the Trapped Negative Space breaks the pattern we are trying to express. As I have heard in many design classes, if you highlight everything, you have highlighted nothing.

> If you highlight everything, you have highlighted nothing.
>
> — Sharon Cave, <u>Sharon Cave Fine Art</u>[104]

 If you see `Negative Space`, like with `THE WALL OF TEXT`, you have done something wrong and need to refine your work.

In this case, it was noticed that the negative space was nicely checker-boarded. Errors do not have meters, and successes have meters but do not have text. It was a simple step to simply collapse the interlocking space.

Next Steps

This chart seems reasonable for expressing the ideas that we want to share with our customers. It is accommodating of diverse biological and digital users and concise enough to convey information quickly.

This is a good start.

This was only a wireframe and a quick sketch to help get a feel for the data that should be presented to users. For example, that header has a lot of Negative Space just screaming to be moved around, and the black grid is overly contrasting, drawing the eye away from the information.

---

[104] Lecture Notes, Sharon Cave Fine Art
https://www.instagram.com/sharoncave61/

Visually, this chart needs a lot of work.

- Marketing design

  This has not even begun to integrate with corporate look and feel. A look at the overall design of the parent reports is necessary.

- Accessibility

  While it has helped to remain constrained to basic accessibility, specialists must look deeper into this.

- Translation

  There is some text, and elements of the text will need to be translated into supported languages.

- Peer review

  This is representative of a single day's work and has not seen a review from peers that may express concerns within our domain.

Having said that, the changes suggested by these various groups will address aesthetic reasoning. We have carefully minimized the overlap between the design and data concerns during the design process. The data is rendered as a simple table, with formatting controlled separately. This means that designers can drastically change the design without significantly changing the data produced.

Again, it's not perfect, but looking toward future cooperation is always necessary, and being open to their suggestions (or sometimes outright changes) can be a wonderful learning experience.

Animation

I remember reading an article by <u>Mike Bostock</u>[105] describing the value of having sorted graph bars slide to their new position when they needed to be changed. Humans see motion and fixate on it, and watching a chart item change position helps us comprehend the change.

This chart (a horizontal bar chart) represents the exact scenario he was describing. We order items by error state (most significant at the top), and using animations to draw attention to changes in order would draw attention to a substantial change in state.

Status

Ⓒ 2023-02-02 15:26

Gov SEC	ⓩ	0.5%
Market NYSE	⚡	1 m ◔
Gov SEDAR	✔	8 h ◔
Market Cboe	✔	7 m ◑
Market CBOT	✔	13 m ◑
Market CHX	✔	4 m ◔

Summary

We were asked, "How will users know the dataset is 'fit for use'?" I think we have achieved that, but we've gone much further

---

[105] Object Constancy, Mike Bostock, https://bost.ocks.org/mike/constancy/#when-constancy-matter

- We have created an advertising list of all our services

- Fit for Use is estimated but left to the user

- It is accommodating of various user needs, <u>offering multiple success paths</u>[106]

- Information density is high but not overwhelming.

- The reduced text allows for it to be used multilingually

- Design and Logic have been <u>separated as concerns</u> for easy collaboration

Not bad for 4 hours after supper, and (frankly) a lot of fun.

I'm hopeful that this cart will make its way in front of our users; I think it will help make our service more visible to new users, offer a lot of information to our current users, and free up the team's time from many status reports.

Ironically, the day after I first presented this report (and wrote most of this post), a colleague gave a presentation on how we present information to users. In it, they emphasized the need to meet the viewers where they are and not complicate the problem. From the online audience, I muted my microphone and burst out laughing. A brief chat between us after the presentation summed up our shared perspective:

Keep it Simple, Stupid

Unfortunately, that's sometimes a complex thing to do.

---

[106] See "Technologic (In)accessibility" for the importance of multiple paths to success

Further Reading

There is so much great reading to be done on how we convey information to users.

 The first stop for me was everything by Mike Bostock. Most famous for his work as a New York Times data visualist, he also invented D3 and Observable HQ. You should read everything you can by him.

 Fundamentals of Data Visualization, by Claus Wilke, is a must-read for anyone interested in visualization and makes an excellent textbook for any classroom

 White Space is Not Your Enemy, by Rebecca Hagen, is a good introduction and foundation into the visual arts from a marketing perspective. This supplies the right level of general theory to apply across several visual disciplines.

 How to Lie with Statistics, by Darrel Huff. Huff focuses on how humans interpret (or misinterpret) numbers and how our expressions of those numbers can help, hurt, or misdirect understanding.

Most importantly, remember that User Experience is more than just rounding the borders of HTML. It's about understanding the psychology, anatomy, and physiology behind our interactions with our users, so make sure you spend time talking to them to understand their experience.

350

Error Message Habituation

Being aware of and mitigating the risks of Habituation in System Maintenance and Design

I will give multiple examples from my career demonstrating the dangers of error message fatigue and habituation leading to ignoring vital signals. Further, they will show how easy it is for humans to fall prey to habituation. Finally, I will conclude with specific techniques and modern tools that can reduce the frequency of its occurrence.

I have three cases rolling around in my head, one from 2004, one from 2012, and one from about three months ago, so it seems I'm doomed to relearn this lesson about once a decade.

As the newly promoted Principle Developer at my first company, I inherited a successful but suffering from growing pains product. The previous Lead had been a graphic designer and had done a wonderful job of building a usable and popular interface, but some of the more engineering aspects had been forgotten along the way. This was reaching a point where it was hampering product growth.

I brought a new perspective on quality and reproducibility, turning the tool from a website into an administrative product. This change in focus between us meant I had years of engineering neglect to catch up on.

A few months later, it wasn't a surprise to me when, one day, the company's owner stormed into the development department angrily and started to rant about a severe defect where data was being dropped. It was a real edge case, and the scenario he was talking about was something I had seen myself, but only rarely and never reproducible. Focused on known issues and bringing the system into a state capable of expanding, I had easily written it off as a ghost in the machine, thrown it on the bug list and pushed it way down. Unfortunately, a customer had seen it this time and could reproduce the issue reliably enough that it had become an embarrassment to the owner, so now it was at the top of the priorities list and became the focus of my exploration.

While I don't remember the exact defect, I remember following the defect into the Web Server's logs (Windows Event Viewer). Previously, my focus had been on the system's external user behaviour, but there were thousands upon thousands of lines of warnings ... every minute in the logs. Warnings about uninitialized variables, unsafe typecasts, and ... a little bit of everything. I had never really given much thought to it because it was so overwhelming as to be meaningless. Still, when I isolated interaction with the form in question and filtered the logs down to just that time frame, *I could consistently see one warning that seemed to relate.*

I'd found my needle in the haystack, but it wasn't an error. It was just a warning among thousands of warnings I had been ignoring. As I dug through the logs, I could see this message appeared regularly when that form was accessed (not always, but regularly). It went back to the very founding of the system (before I had even started my programming education, I was still a nurse). This error had been getting reported for almost a decade, and nobody had seen it for two reasons:

1. it was a warning, not an error

2. the signal had been lost in a sea of noise

I learned a valuable lesson that day. No Warnings, No Errors became my mantra.

Naturally, I first fixed the issue that had been spotted, but this defect had been signalled by a warning in the system logs that if someone had addressed it, we would have fixed it almost a decade before. So, I started to address **all** the warnings in the logs.

Most were relatively benign, identifying (perhaps) that a variable had not been explicitly initialized before use. Still, since null was treated as a zero or empty string, it didn't impact the system's behaviour. But as I made minor corrections and the log volume reduced, some of the warnings started taking on more ominous tones. More system defects were identified (and corrected), and most significantly to me, an actual error started to present regularly ... One that had been missed in the excessive volume in the logs.

So, what was the core of the lesson?

Seeing a large volume of errors can make us insensitive to them. When we ignore significant messages, we train ourselves to not pay attention, and that's when bad things happen.

 The term habituation is used in several related contexts, including medical, social, and psychological. Still, the general summary would be the loss of recognition of negative stimuli due to repeated (habitual) exposure to them

We see this all around us and in our day-to-day lives. People get habituated to getting yelled at by a peer, becoming numb to the exposure. Physically, a carpenter may become desensitized to getting slivers, simply pulling them out at the end of the day rather than immediately flinching. I like a hot shower, but it usually takes a moment for my skin to get used to the hot water. It has even been documented in plants; the Mimosa Pudica is known to flinch when touched but will stop flinching with repeated touching.

This helps us get on with life.

Flinching is a critical reflexive reaction that protects us from bad things happening. Stubbing your toe **should** produce an immediate "protect your toe" response; getting an unexpected cut on your hand is **dangerous**, and I **should** jerk my hand back from scalding water; but sometimes the cut is minor and expected (slivers) and for the most part just part of the job ... life has to go on. A hot shower is a significant temperature change, but it isn't harmful and is rather pleasant once I get used to it. The process of habituation allows us to maintain our high-alert state while at the same time learning to moderate it under various conditions.

Humans are biologically queued to become habituated. It is part of our survival strategy as a species. It's built into you.

Therefore, you cannot ignore the risk of habituation to our systems.

Receiving an error signal (error messages, warnings, failing tests) regularly, evaluating it as safe to ignore, and not taking action psychologically prepare you to ignore it later. It begins to habituate you to the error signal, placing it on a pile of things we can ignore.

Common Examples of Programmer Error Habituation

I have found examples of error habituation at every organization I have ever worked at and in every role I have filled. They do not always present the same way, but they are pervasive throughout the industry, even presenting themselves as Best Practices to the untrained eye.

Errors and Warnings

This is the most obvious since it's right in the name, which makes it a good place to start.

- Compiler warnings

- System Log Warnings

- Pager notifications

This was my first exposure to this. We learn through practice at school that compiler errors prevent us from submitting our assignments, but warnings do not. With the short intensity of student life, ignoring warnings becomes a habitual survival strategy. As we become mature professionals, we learn that these messages were put in place to convey meaning to us and offer us protection.

Known Software Defects

Defects in software are discovered, and discovering and correcting them is the art form. In the words of Robert Glass:

> 43. Maintenance is a solution, not a problem
>
> — Facts and Fallacies of Software Engineering[107]

It is important to realize that defects must be expected and worked on. At the same time, there is always more work than time, so some form of prioritization is necessary. This means we must ignore them for a while (even if it is just the time it takes to fix them).

The problem is that the more defects we acknowledge are present, the more we tend to ignore them as irrelevant. The more we defer fixing bugs, the more we get into the habit of deferring bug fixes.

TODO and Change Comments

TODO comments within the code were a way to identify an item that needs to be addressed; we'll come back to this later.

There is a strong likelihood that we are ignoring the problem because we are busy with something else. Certainly, it is impossible to split ourselves into two to address both issues simultaneously, so note the secondary problem. In contrast, we address the primary one that makes sense.

The problem arises when we don't come back to it.

---

[107] Facts and Fallacies of Software Engineering, Robert Glass
https://www.amazon.ca/Facts-Fallacies-Software-Engineering-Robert/dp/0321117425?

Accumulating `TODO` notes through code can become excessive noise, causing us to start ignoring the message. Further, as these are usually listed along with the warnings and errors, they represent noise that drowns out more important signals.

Do not become habituated to seeing useless comments.

A header in an individual file containing a list of every change ever made to the file is a typical pattern that has become an anti-pattern. The purpose of these comments is to offer a log of changes that have been made to the code in their contextual place.

Unfortunately, this (good) habit started decades ago with different coding styles. The pattern assumes that a single file is self-contained to all its changes and does not interact with other entities (since recognized as a faulty assumption). There is also the problem that decades of messages accumulating at the start of the file means an impenetrable `WALL-OF-TEXT` must be scrolled past before anything meaningful can begin. This immediate scroll past habituates us to perceive large blocks of comments as meaningless when we should consider large explanations in the code something important and meaningful.

What started as a good idea for small files over short time frames has evolved into a bad idea with better alternatives.

Relearning the Lesson (Twice)

A decade later, I found myself on contract with a major corporation that had terminated its previous contracting company due to poor quality performance. My team had been hired to not only deliver but also do it with an eye to quality.

On my first day reading the regression test suite, I naturally glanced at the warning list to see how many warnings were in the code. I immediately found myself staring at a list of hundreds of warnings and thousands of TODO messages. Naturally, I tried to ignore them... they were things that needed to be done in the future, not immediately. However, as I cleared the significant backlog of warnings, I started to come across the TODOs' locations.

It was horrifying.

```
@Test
public void ReallyImportantThing() {
   //TODO: implement this
   Assert.assertTrue(true);
}
```

In many (most) cases, the note suggested a person should implement the test for real. (There is a similar story, I thought, told by Spolsky, of a notorious function implementation in MS Office ... the same thing)

In my case, I suspect the previous team, under pressure to perform and deliver, had been masking gaps for a long time. Many regression tests were simple stubs that returned a success no matter what. This allowed them to claim the job was done while promising themselves they would fix it ... later ... when they had time. That time never came.

It was difficult to explain to the client that I was taking a week to reevaluate how much testing was actually being performed. When I reduced their test count by more than half, I needed to remind them they had hired us specifically because they knew there had been a problem. Identifying those problems and giving honest assessments is where our value comes from.

TODOs were added to my list of things not permitted in code bases I was involved in.

No Warnings, No Errors

Another decade has passed, and recently (weeks), I had to catch myself again.

I implemented a basic continuous monitoring alert system on a new system we are working on. It periodically scans the system for invalid states and immediately notifies the team of the bad state (OK, it informs me and one other, and we notify the larger team ... baby steps). If an alert is issued, we must act to save the system.

I ignored a message.

In this case, the alert was to notify us that we had stopped receiving signals from a remote source, and I had ignored it. As a batch process, it is not uncommon for the source process to take longer than anticipated. This isn't a big deal since usually, it delivers shortly after we check, and we just pick it up on the next pass.

Except it is a big deal because I ignored it.

My colleague, just returning from vacation, called me and asked if I had noticed that the system was erroring, she didn't see a ticket and wondered if I was dealing with it. I told her it was no big deal, that one fails regularly ... and as the words came out of my mouth, I heard what I had just said.

Sure enough, we looked closer, and the failure occurred for three cycles; the source was not transmitting data, and I, through habituation, ignored the failure.

Preventing Habituation

There is really only one solution to preventing error habituation: address every error, warning, or notice and treat it immediately and with the utmost priority.

While I say this, there are some subtleties to how we achieve this:

1. Always fix defects before implementing new features

2. Never ignore a defect message

Various tools are available to help us address this and various mentalities.

Errors that can be ignored

There is no such thing as a reported error that can be ignored.

1. the system is in an invalid state and needs to be fixed immediately or

2. the error notification system is flawed and needs to be fixed immediately

Incorrect notifications could be a log monitor that alerts when an invalid state is encountered. Upon inspection, the state is determined to be undesirable (not invalid). We'll ignore the error; it will correct itself later.

NO! Change the log monitor to take into account the new information. It needs to be run less frequently and count how long the error state exists (waiting before alerting), but whatever gave you a reason to think it can be ignored needs to be incorporated into the official rules for alerting.

Failing Tests

As previously mentioned, you can't be working on two problems simultaneously in two places simultaneously. One problem must be set aside while you focus on the other. Unfortunately, this leads to ignoring errors, which becomes habitual.

To avoid this, the first step is to create a task in your backlog, which immediately gives us a record of the issue. Secondly, we should immediately generate an automated test that can allow us to reproduce the error. The problem is that the test will be failing, constantly reporting an error to us. This is a failure signal that we want to ignore (probably using a SKIP) until we get the defect fixed; we immediately mark it as skip, an ignore status.

This is a problem.

 We can resolve this by having a team rule that all SKIP tests **MUST**[108] have a ticket number associated with them and addressing **every** skip during **every** planning meeting. For me, this often takes the form of reporting skips without ticket numbers, as fails and fails must be

---

[108] RFC-2119, Key words for use in RFCs to Indicate Requirement Levels. Defines the interpretation of keywords in engineering specifications. https://www.rfc-editor.org/rfc/rfc2119.html

addressed immediately. Skips with a ticket link directly to their ticket in their reporting.

Lastly, the team **MAY** implement a <u>zero defects policy</u>[109]. This is an agreement with the business that defects will be fixed before <u>new features are implemented</u>[110].

> **NOTE**
>
> I have never been satisfied with the reports generated by testing systems, and I have always written custom visualizations to track defects. This has had the side effect of my introducing concepts like adding extra states to TestNG's default reporting (`known`, `manual`, `feature`) with active links to the repository and issue tracking software.

Comments Calling for Action

`TODO` comments were a classic way to express something you need to come back to and finish something off, and they still have their place, but fundamentally, they are a call to ignore the problem (but only for now).

The problem here is the same as with all the others; we need a way to prevent it from becoming forever.

---

[109] Zero Defect Mentality: History and Steps to Zero Defects Manufacturing, Renaud Anjoran, 2021-07-09 https://www.cmc-consultants.com/blog/zero-defect-mentality-implementations-and-history

[110] Zero Defects Philosophy in Software Development Environment, Agile Development https://www.agiledevelopment.org/agile-talk/134-zero-defects-in-software-development

A straightforward way of handling this is to put a Version Control hook in your repository that prevents check-ins of TODO comments. Generally, you should only put this on protected branches. This allows you to put them in your code to enable you to continue working but prevents you from submitting them to the official branch by accident. Forcing you to finish the job you planned on doing. If you can't get to a TODO, don't leave it in the code; register it in the backlog as something that still needs doing. This leaves the alert list available for warnings and errors so they don't get hidden.

Those massive headers at the beginning of the code only work to mask issues. They get in the way of text searches and require a lot of visual space to scroll past. All that is for something that is based on an old paradigm: changes are constrained to a single file.

Modern VCS tools assume that a change may require the context of several locations in code to be meaningful and have logging built into them. Keep your changes in the Change System database, reducing the visual noise by placing them in a contextual list that is hidden until you need them. When you need them, the list is optimally indexed for what it is.

Conclusion

As humans, we make mistakes. Each decision we make is a totally new decision that we must make, injecting the opportunity for error. This opportunity for error can be compounded by biases introduced from our experience. Habituation of errors represents a biasing of our behaviour that we are biologically predisposed toward and can be dangerous to our work.

It is important that we, as professionals, work to overcome these dangerous biases through constant diligence and self-appraisal.

As software developers, our work captures decision-making before the stimulus and action, and defects can have catastrophic effects. Teaching ourselves to ignore benign errors can mask more catastrophic issues that have a significant impact on people's lives:

 Aeroplanes <u>fall out of the sky</u>

 Small business owners get <u>falsely accused and imprisoned</u>

Further Reading

I hope I've made the case that it is easy to teach ourselves to ignore errors because we are humans, and humans are fallible. Addressing this is hard but not new.

<u>Facts and Fallacies of Software Engineering</u> (Robert L. Glass)

 is a great read that opened my eyes to how common these issues are and how we all want things to be true, even when they aren't. I keep a copy of the table of contents in a text file, just so I can search it regularly.

Downfall: The Case against Boeing (Netflix)

 discusses an important event in computing history. Remember that in 1969, Software saved an aircraft with a bad attitude sensor, while in 2018, Software killed 318 people due to a bad attitude sensor.

Any YouTube video on Aircraft crash investigations

 Observe how multiple people must ignore warning signs for a long time for a problem to occur. Note how easy it is for dangerous behaviour to become habituated.

Consider reading the manuals of your favourite tool suite to get a better understanding of why the software was developed, how it is meant to help you, and how it can replace some practices you may have thought were a good idea

 Test Suites can help you identify errors methodically

 Project Management tools can help prioritize and track outstanding issues

 Version Control Systems can help you understand why historical changes were made, offering a significant amount of context when you need it. I actually

recommend reading <u>SVN's manual</u> as it brought a substantial paradigm shift at the time it was introduced that needed to be explained (Use Git, read about SVN)

... and always pay attention to your own emotions and biases... your mistakes are always available to learn from.

Maintaining Privacy in Data Shares

A Guide to Big Data Privacy for Dummy Developers

- Balancing the power of modern computational capabilities with individual privacy is a formidable challenge in data sharing.

- Benevolent actors, in their quest for insights, may inadvertently breach privacy by applying multiple dimensions to data and exposing individuals.

- Introducing a privacy metric to mechanically measure the risk associated with shared datasets, aiding in decision-making for responsible data sharing.

When we delve into the intricacies of data sharing, one paramount consideration arises — privacy. The very essence of privacy hinges on how informative the shared data is, necessitating a quantifiable approach.

In today's information-gathering landscape, the sheer capacity often leaves one in awe. Privacy and data ethics, perennially debated topics, trace their roots back 250 years to the US Constitution's Fourth Amendment, which asserts the right to be secure in personal papers against unreasonable searches and seizures. This is just one significant example of recognizing the perils of exposing personal information to authorities.

Long suspected, a revelation in 2013 confirmed governmental organizations, such as the NSA's, information capabilities to the forefront. The revelation that the NSA accumulates every phone call from every individual was not just mind-boggling; it raised significant questions about privacy and data ethics. The sheer scale of data collection raised concerns about the potential misuse and the safeguards in place.

We're not talking about datasets reminiscent of the Access Databases of the 1990s for mailing lists; these are colossal databases maintained by governments and mega-corporations. They harbour the potential to craft exact profiles of individuals. When amalgamated, the sheer volume of data generated by individuals provides a unique perspective on the individual[111].

---

[111] `K68mPpQOmdxPfzQtgikKaw==`. This value is generated from my browser settings. It allows my online activity to be uniquely tracked across multiple websites and without the assistance of cookies. What's your fingerprint? https://fingerprintjs.github.io/fingerprintjs/

How do we balance the power of modern computational capabilities with the privacy of the individuals whose data we collect?

The Road to Hell is Paved with Good Intentions

There are many layers to security, but often, the first that should be applied is to guard against misuse: legitimate users use the data for inappropriate purposes.

In movies, a private investigator will buy information from an informant; super-spies are seen breaking into vaults to steal information about an individual. These are not complete fabrications; I have been involved in several investigations regarding personal information leaks. I have been involved in at least two cases of data theft (both as a Nurse and as a Data Professional); in both cases, a private investigator hired an insider to look up information in the system. In both cases, gathering evidence to trace the activity was as simple as looking up data access logs that did not align with business duties but did align with the suspected misuse. The system's mechanics were sufficient to restrict, identify, and enforce access to data.

Data Warehouses and modern analytics add a wrinkle to this problem.

Data Warehouses can be compelling information resources. Depending on your business line, they will contain all the joined data and personal information of customers and employees across multiple business lines. For governmental organizations like the NSA, the customer data points are the citizenry and visitors to the country. This is a potent tool for analysis; however, it carries risks of misuse.

Mechanically, the nature of the bulk data that is being shared makes it vulnerable to misuse by benign, malicious, and (most importantly) benevolent actors.

- Keeping malicious actors out is obvious: do security background checks to find honest people, hire honest people, and create guidelines for use that honest people can follow.

- Benign actors are ... well ... benign. They are the honest people you hire and are happy to follow corporate policies like: You must not look up yourself, your friends, or your family.

- Benevolent actors are more complicated.

If we have screened for honest people, we have biased our search for helpful people. Combine that with large datasets and the fact that data analysts are curious people, and we have a recipe for disaster.

The benefit is derived from performing aggregate analysis on many detailed values. If an organization has sensitive data, but an honest analyst can offer some significant insight by inspecting it, they will make the data available to the Analyst. This generally takes the form of the Analyst proposing their study, describing their data needs, and then sending them the data that aligns with their request.

... and this is where it starts to fall apart ...

A reasonable request for data may exist within the United States Census Bureau[112] to create a report identifying a gender wage gap.

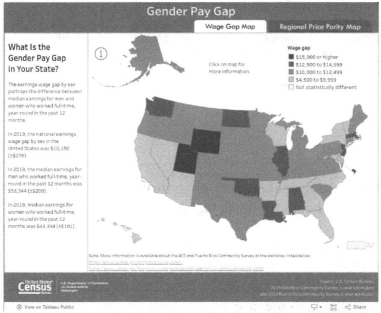

A United States Census Bureau data visualization regarding the gender wage gap by US state available online

To support the request, the analyst is given access to a dataset containing all tax filings for the past dozen years. The analyst then loads the data into the analysis tool of their choice, does a simple sum by state and sees their results.

---

[112] What Is the Gender Wage Gap in Your State?, United Census Bureau, Megan Wisniewski, 2022-03-01. Contains an excellent example of a valuable analysis.
https://www.census.gov/library/stories/2022/03/what-is
-the-gender-wage-gap-in-your-state.html

```
select
  year,
  state,
  sum(case when gender = 'M' then income else 0 end)
    / sum(case when gender = 'M' then 1 else 0 end)
    as avgM,
  sum(case when gender = 'W' then income else 0 end)
    / sum(case when gender = 'W' then 1 else 0 end)
    as avgW,
  sum(income)/count(*) as avg
from
  dataset
group by
  state, year
```

Their manager approves hitting the publish button, and the team heads for lunch together.

Over lunch, the original author is discussing their findings with their colleagues when someone asks a simple question:

I wonder if age has anything to do with that?

That's an interesting question and may be useful to add to analysis reports. So the Analyst goes back to their favourite tool. The data is still in the analysis tool, and all they have to do is adjust the parameters of the query.... This is where informational security starts to break down. This is not what the data was authorized to be used for.

While this is a benign example, each data dimension brings us closer to revealing the individual. In their rush to discover meaningful insights, the Analyst has applied two dimensions to the individual in question. While this may not be a big deal at the state level, imagine applying filters like this to the town of Albertville, which has a population of 86. Suddenly, using age may be unique enough to distinguish some individuals, and publishing their wages to their neighbours could cause bad-blood in town.

The security (privacy) of customer data is of paramount importance. It requires measuring the information about the individual we are sharing. This concept of revealing the individual effectively that of information entropy. Entropy is a measure of the amount of surprise; in this case, it is the amount of surprise we have when we discover the actual person.

Aside from purely mechanical safeguards like network access controls, encryption, and permission, we need to consider the possibility of shared data being misused. The ultimate security tool is to simply not share data we do not want people to have access to or (more importantly) to control the context in which the data is interpreted. This allows us to maintain a high level of entropy around the individual.

Whenever someone asks for access, we must evaluate whether we are exposing enough information to expose the individual.

This requires human thought and analysis, and humans make mistakes. Overworked, over-tired, or pressured by the office bully, a human may give permission to expose more data than is appropriate, allowing researchers to dox an individual accidentally. Some mechanism for mechanically, automatically, and unbiasedly measuring the privacy risk of a proposed dataset is necessary because...

Hell truly is paved with good intentions[113].

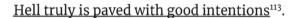

[113] Hell's Gate (Darvas Crater) was created when someone threw a match in with the good intention of stopping a gas leak. Darvas Crater
https://en.wikipedia.org/wiki/Darvaza_gas_crater

The Problem

To best understand the problem, let us consider a simplified example.

ID	SSN	Name	Gender	Email	Income	Country
3Pyib5FZAQ	969228228	Joyce Lindsay	♀	alice@example.com	$77,504	USA
FCF9dVnFbP	660379912	Rocky Sree	♂	dude948@example.com	$37,201	USA
E4BXl1iWdI	810707343	Nona Romy	▽	ci@example.com	$23,159	USA
ix7WxIC2GV	258325821	Joyce Sree	▽	sree@example.com	$46,746	USA

By studying this dataset, we can see that it is a basic income data set for US citizens. It includes some demographic information like their name and gender, as well as some contact information. While it does have a random identifier, it also contains their Social Security Number, something we do not want to just hand out to the first Private Investigator who asks for it.

Our goal is to give information to customers (analysts) who request it and ensure we do not provide so much that we expose the individual. We can define this as

> **the information given to the analyst must not be sufficient to identify a single individual**

The very first step is to remove the account identifiers. We don't want those handed out, but the rest of the data is unclear. What data does the Analyst need to satisfy their research needs?

Our customer is studying income, so we *must* include that, but the concern would be that it gets exposed. While the individual might recognize their income, assuming they've kept that private, it should stay private and not be associated with them.

Let's start by considering the email address. Email addresses are designed to be unique to the individual. Let's give our customers the dataset with only an email address and an income. We have effectively tied the income to that person. On the other hand, exposing the country does not tell us anything unique about the individual (everyone in our dataset is from the USA). So, if we are going to share data, we want to share data we want to share data with minimal impact.

Our Analyst studying gender inequality (Alice) is doing pretty well, having only asked for gender and income.

ID	Gender	Income
A1	⚲	$77,504
A2	☌	$37,201
A3	▽	$23,159
A4	▽	$46,746

Another analyst, a couple of desks over (Bob), has been working on an algorithm for a while and thinks he can use Last Name as a proxy for race. He would like to do a study using names and incomes. The Privacy analyst, on the ball, notices that full names are perfectly unique, so he offers a list containing only last names.

ID	FamName	Race (Calculated)	Income
B9	Lindsay	SkyBlue-Pink	$77,504
B8	Romy	SkyBlue-Pink	$23,159
B7	Sree	Marine Mammal	$37,201
B6	Sree	Marine Mammal	$46,746

Alice and Bob are discussing their findings over lunch one day when their co-worker Eve overhears them. Eve's ears perk up because she is also a Private investigator who is always looking for exciting datasets and surreptitiously acquires the two datasets.

Eve knows she has acquired something useless: the two datasets have been vetted to ensure that the individuals involved cannot be uniquely identified. However, with closer inspection, she notes that the incomes are unique. Using this insight, she joins the two tables.

Alice	Bob	Sal (Calculated)	FamName	Gender	Race	Income
A1	B9	Mx.	Lindsay	⊕	SkyBlue-Pink	$77,504
A3	B8	Mr.	Romy	○	SkyBlue-Pink	$23,159
A2	B7	Ms.	Sree	▽	Marine Mammal	$37,201
A4	B6	Ms.	Sree	▽	Marine Mammal	$46,746

Eve has achieved an interesting effect. She has not only joined the two original datasets to get a more complete picture, but she has also constructed likely salutations that are new data that exceed the scope of either of the original datasets. While it is not a complete picture, she has started to build a profile on individuals. These profiles can be used for purposes that exceed the original permitted use of the data.

A Real Risk

While this story is obviously made up, it is not unrealistic. If one looks at the way we package modern reports, one can see that these risks are present everywhere.

Modern data presentations demand some level of interactivity. The ability to filter, change, and compare the data on the fly is a powerful and compelling tool. But there is a risk. To share these visualizations and make them dynamic, we have to ensure sufficient detail is embedded in the data we are sharing.

That data is in the file; just because you don't know how to extract it doesn't mean nobody does. For the tool to be useful, some people do know how[114] ... that's how they make the visualizations work.

Like Alice and Bob, we act with the best intentions but easily become Eve, sharing data inappropriately if we aren't careful. We share data with too little entropy and hide it behind a mask.

What Can We Do?

For people concerned with individual privacy, this is bad. So the question becomes, as custodians, how can we prevent it?

While human thought and analysis will always be necessary, they are subject to bias, inconsistency, and mistakes. Automating or offering automated decision-making aids to humans is always a good idea. In light of this need, can we develop a metric to measure the level of privacy in our shared datasets? Can this metric aid in the decision-making process around data share approvals?

---

[114] How to read in tableau (twbx) file into python, Stackoverflow. Describes how to open and read a Tableau file with no specialty tools. Like so many file types, its just a zip file with the data in a plain text file. https://stackoverflow.com/questions/48634674/how-to-read-in-tableau-twbx-file-into-python

Increase the Entropy

There are a few normal practices we can follow to increase the entropy of the data. In our example, the two innocent datasets were joined using unique income.

Initially, `income` was allowed because it was necessary, but that created the vulnerability. We can increase the entropy of the field by rounding it to some level.

Do we need it to be accurate to the dollar? What about the thousandth of a dollar?

In doing so, we increase the number of people who will match the value and protect their anonymity.

Measure the Entropy

If we can measure the entropy, we should. Rather than leaving it to custodians to use their best judgment, we can offer them a way to objectively measure the state.

This metric can be made visible to both requesters and approvers to help them decide the appropriateness of the request. We can estimate the entropy of the request before it is even approved, allowing us to keep safety at the forefront of our minds. Later, we can measure the entropy of the request to ensure it is sufficiently anonymized before releasing it to the public.

Create Versatile Environments

Don't dictate; cooperate.

One of the risks mentioned early in our example was the Analyst's holding on to the data. We produce the safe dataset and then make it available to the Analyst for loading into their tool of choice.

This is a common story: we have powerful computers and tools we've trained on. These tools have power, but they carry the risk of moving data off of the controlled environments.

By creating powerful and versatile environments, we allow customers to do their analysis in a controlled environment. We should also accommodate the needs of experts and create environments capable of accommodating those experts' diverse needs.

This passively discourages requests to take the data off-system by giving them access to the tools they want.

Further Reading

 C.E. Shannon, <u>Mathematical Theory of Communication</u>, 1948. Shannon created the idea of informational entropy and developed a way to measure it

How To Quantify Privacy Protection in Shared Datasets

An Entropy-Based Approach for Objective Evaluation and Automated Approval

We will discuss tools for estimating and automating privacy enforcement in datasets.

- **Objective Data Privacy Evaluation**: Discuss a straightforward approach using objective measures to gauge and improve data privacy in shared datasets.

- **Estimating Data Privacy Levels**: Learn through real-world examples how estimating data privacy levels can be a powerful tool, minimizing bias and enhancing informed decision-making

- **Automated Checks for Enhanced Workflow**: Explore the application of automated checks in the approval workflow to simplify processes and boost productivity in safeguarding sensitive information

 A working example is available on ObservableHQ where you can see the calculations for yourself as well as try different parameters.

In the previous chapter, we discussed the importance and challenges of preserving privacy, underscoring the critical nature of cautious information sharing. This principle extends beyond safeguarding personal identities to shielding covert subjects like structures, military units, and other sensitive entities. The guiding rule is clear: the less revealed, the better.

Implementing this principle poses a formidable challenge. Over-sharing risks exposing individuals and jeopardizes the confidentiality of various subjects. Assessing the privacy of shared datasets demands meticulous effort. Privacy analysts invest time scrutinizing datasets[115][116], applying rules, and leveraging professional judgment to ensure the concealment of both personal and classified subjects.

However, relying solely on subjective analysis has its inherent risks. Analysts, being human, are susceptible to biases, fatigue, and external pressures, occasionally leading to lapses in judgment. Despite these challenges, there's a growing need to share data for diverse benefits.

The predicament endures: how do we establish a threshold for sharing information without compromising the privacy of individuals or the secrecy of sensitive subjects? How can we alleviate the burden of the privacy evaluators while simultaneously ensuring that shared data doesn't pose excessive risks?

---

[115] Data Privacy Handbook, Utrecht University
https://utrechtuniversity.github.io/dataprivacyhandbook/research-scenarios.html
[116] Data Privacy Handbook, Utrecht University
https://utrechtuniversity.github.io/dataprivacyhandbook/faq.html

Enter Claude Shannon's Information Entropy concept, originating from The Mathematical Theory of Communication in 1949. Shannon's concept of the smallest piece of indivisible information provides a quantifiable measure of data. This measure is not only applicable to personal privacy but also to the confidentiality of secret subjects. It furnishes an objective metric to estimate the privacy risk associated with exposing a dataset, serving as a valuable tool for analysts and automated systems in assessing risks related to personal and classified information.

These concepts present a practical tool for striking a balance between safeguarding subjects' privacy and the imperative to share data for analysis.

Definitions

To ensure precision and clarity, I have substituted the term "individual" with the more inclusive "subject". While my primary focus revolves around protecting people's privacy, it's crucial to recognize that some fields manage data of a covert nature that extends beyond human entities. Examples include tight holes[117] in the oil and gas sector, covert police and military locations, and discreetly insured and transported tangible objects[118].

---

[117] SLB, Energy Glossary. tight hole. A well that the operator requires be kept as secret as possible, especially the geologic information. Exploration wells, especially rank wildcats, are often designated as tight.
https://glossary.slb.com/en/Terms/t/tight_hole.aspx
[118] New details about $20M Toronto airport gold heist revealed in Brink's suit against Air Canada, National Post, 2023-10-10
https://nationalpost.com/news/toronto/new-details-toronto-pearson-airport-gold-heist

Remarkably, the strategies for privacy protection can be universally applied, regardless of the nature of the subject.

Central to our exploration is the concept of privacy, which we define as the resistance to deducing the individual's identity. Think of it like the classic game of <u>Guess Who?</u>[119] where your opponent uses provided data to guess the subject's identity and then uses a broader dataset to gather more information. Decreased privacy erodes when data boosts our confidence in identifying individuals, while increased privacy comes from a lower confidence level in distinguishing one individual from another.

It's crucial to emphasize that privacy isn't only preserved by obscuring a person's name or ID. Even with fabricated labels for the subject, comprehensive knowledge about them can still lead to privacy breaches. As an analogy, personal privacy can be compromised even if you know everything about a subject but refer to them by a pseudonym, much like my limited knowledge about my neighbour, whom I simply recognize as "that lady next door".

There are three significant roles in any informational message transfer: the sender, the receiver, and a potential interceptor. In the case of a shared dataset, we find these three actors present. Privacy Analysts sit between our source data and filter it, acting like a sender, sending a sanitized message out. The intended recipient is a Data Analyst, whether an internal colleague or a member of the public. Lastly, the Data Analyst could be a malicious actor, either gaining access to the data nefariously or, more pertinently, using a permitted dataset in a nefarious way.

---

[119] Guess Who Board Game
https://www.amazon.ca/Original-Guessing-Double-Sided-Character-Families/dp/B09WX9KT3S/

While entropy is often linked with the predictability of physical systems, it can be better understood as a measure of chaos. Information Entropy, similar to the concept of chaos, quantifies the level of surprise within a system. In a stable or predictable state, a system exhibits high entropy. Consequently, possessing complete knowledge about a subject leaves minimal room for surprise; conversely, knowing nothing allows for unexpected discoveries.

While Claude Shannon is renowned for the `bit`, several names and related measures apply to the same concept of information entropy. The `shannon` measure represents the most minor, indivisible unit of information, a binary state (`true` or `false`) synonymous with a `bit` (or binary digit). This concept builds on previous work defining the `hartley` (Ralph Hartley, 1929), which uses a decimal base and can also be referred to as the dit, among other terms used by Turing, Good, and others.

An Example

An example is likely useful in explaining how to enforce privacy through an automated mechanism. Samples often help us orient ourselves to the task at hand. Naturally, in a discussion about privacy, we will want a dataset with individuals whose privacy we will want to protect. Still, we also want to ensure these individuals are not representative of anyone real. To achieve this, we have downloaded a sample customer dataset from <u>Sling Academy</u>[120], which gives us a list of individuals and some personal information about them.

---

[120] Customers Sample Data, Sling Academy
https://www.slingacademy.com/article/customers-sampl e-data-csv-json-xml-and-xlsx/

I've also cleaned the data to make it a little more suitable for our purposes, primarily by adding some randomized identifiers, introducing some `nulls`, and removing extraneous characters.

	id	ssn	first_name	last_name	email	ph
	string ▾	string ▾	string ▾	string ▾	string ▾	str
	1,000 unique values	1,000 unique values	uni	uniqu	1,000 unique values	1,
			353 categories	487 categories		
0	5p97dl8jmlr	611786456	Joseph	Rice	josephrice131@example	18(
1	s41q2tb5h3	395178457	Gary	Moore	garymoore386@example	22]
2	41hdgnm4v13	992475463	John	Walker	johnwalker944@example	38[
3	3mld4gpns1	963777567	Eric	Carter	ericcarter176@example.	451
4	5inrjirotep	912404513	William	Jackson	williamjackson427@exar	62!
5	1np44e2knjd	735188205	Nicole	Jones	nicolejones228@exampl	178
6	47dfsg7s9n9	957957326	David	Davis	daviddavis980@example	06]
7	3toogm2jlb5	407462840	Jason	Montgomery	jasonmontgomery889@e	00]
8	42knacdbmv1	415420996	Kent	Weaver	kentweaver695@exampl	00(
9	4hv8f6s1vc3	196389163	Darrell	Dillon	darrelldillon573@exampl	15(

Q Search

The base data used includes 1000 rows from a sample customer set

We have 1000 rows representing data you may find in sales, lending, or social welfare domains. Each row represents one customer with a unique ID for each person, a large random number we assign as a primary key. The individual's social security number and name are present to further identify them. We also have general contact information (phone, email), demographic information (gender, job), and some facts that are meaningful to the business (number of sales and total sales dollars). Note that gender uses the public toilet symbols for woman (○), man (▽), and neutral (⊘) as mandated by several <u>US</u> <u>States</u>[121].

Looking more closely at some of these fields, we might notice that the values inside our fields have different

---

[121] Solving The Mysteries Of The California Restroom Sign, Certified Access Specialist Institute https://casinstitute.org/article/solving-mysteries-california-restroom-sign

associated frequencies. If we consider gender, we can see that there are only 3 possible values and that, for the most part, knowing about them does not tell us much about the individual. For example, if I tell you that our subject is a man, you only have a 1 in 508 chance of guessing who that person is. If, on the other hand, I tell you the subject's first name is "David", you have a much better chance of identifying the subject (1 in 17 chance).

Field	Category	Freq	Prob	Privacy
string ▾	string ▾	integer ▾	number ▾ {}	number ▾ {}
all values: "gender"	3 unique values			
		0 · · · 600	0 · · · 0.15	850m · · · 1
gender	▽	508	0.002	0.998
gender	○	484	0.002	0.998
gender	♀	8	0.125	0.875

The probability of guessing an individual by their gender depends on which gender is exposed

This ability to measure predictability brings us close to Claude Shannon's definition of entropy, or surprise. Given the probability of guessing the person, we can also calculate the amount of surprise. By calculating the probability of randomly selecting an individual from within each category, we can get an idea of how private the field is.

In our case, the chosen field, `gender`, has 3 categories. By taking an average of their probabilities (`0.0430`), we get a general sense of their level of privacy.

We can repeat this for all fields, giving us a privacy profile for the dataset.

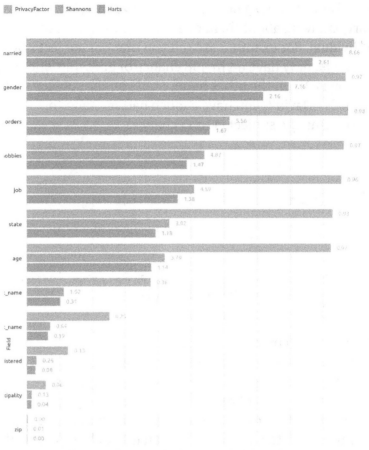

Legend: PrivacyFactor, Shannons, Harts

Fields (top to bottom):
- married: 8.66, 2.61
- gender: 0.97, 7.16, 2.16
- orders: 0.98, 5.56, 1.67
- hobbies: 0.97, 4.87, 1.47
- job: 0.96, 4.59, 1.38
- state: 0.93, 3.92, 1.18
- age: 0.94, 3.79, 1.14
- _name: 0.16, 1.02, 0.31
- _name: 0.24, 0.64, 0.19
- istered: 0.13, 0.26, 0.08
- cipality: 0.04, 0.13, 0.04
- zip: 0.00, 0.01, 0.00

Measures of privacy for each field as a probability, Shannon, or Hart

The privacy factor calculated for each field matches our intuition: perfectly unique IDs carry a very low privacy factor, and items like `first_name` are relatively anonymous. Having observed this, we can observe some non-intuitive findings, such as the very low privacy associated with `municipality`. We also have a cautionary reminder: emails and phone numbers are unique to people.

```
// Calculate the privacy profile of all the fields
PrivacyProfile = (function(){ return {
    "hashed": null,
  table: Object.entries(fields1).map(d=>{
    let key = d[0];
    d = d[1];
    let total = d.total;

    let categories = Object.values(d.values).length;
    let privFactor = Object.values(d.values)
      .map(freq=>1-(1/freq))
      .reduce((a,d)=>a+d,0)
      /categories
      ;
    let shannon = Object.values(d.values)
      .map(freq=>Math.log(freq)/Math.LN2)
      .reduce((a,d)=>a+d,0)
      /categories
      ;
    let hart = Object.values(d.values)
      .map(freq=>Math.log(freq)/Math.LN10)
      .reduce((a,d)=>a+d,0)
      /categories
      ;
    return {
      "Field": key,
      "PrivacyFactor": privFactor,
      "Shannons": shannon,
      "Harts": hart,
      "Probability": 1-privFactor,
      "Values": total,
      "Categories" : categories,
    };
  })
}})();
```

Applying the Measure to whole datasets

If our goal is to retain privacy while sharing data in a large-scale environment, we can use this as a tool. Rather than relying purely on people's subjective judgement, we can *aid* their judgement with an objective measure. When a data analyst comes to the Privacy Team looking for access to sensitive data, we can measure the privacy level of their data request.

We can calculate the net privacy of a request by taking a cumulative product of the privacy factors of the individual fields being requested.

Intuitively, we can immediately see that the *entire* dataset offers little to no privacy; however, this can be more formally stated by taking the product of all the fields.

```
PrivacyProfile.table.reduce((a,d)=>{
  return a * d.PrivacyFactor
},0);
```

With items like the SSN, some items are 0 privacy, and including these in the product results in a Net Privacy Factor of "no privacy" (hard zero: 0)

 We should expect a Data Request to <u>be only for the data required for the analysis</u>[122]. Therefore, the request should include a reduced set. To perform this calculation on demand, we can create a generic function.

---

[122] Sharing data with collaborators, Data Privacy Handbook, Utrecht University https://utrechtuniversity.github.io/dataprivacyhandbook/data-sharing-collaboration.html

```
function GenerateReqest(req = null){
  // if nothing specific was requested,
  //make this a randomized selection
  if(!req){
    let fldprob = Math.ceil(
      PrivacyProfile.table.length * Math.random()
      ) / PrivacyProfile.length
      ;
    req = PrivacyProfile.table
      .filter(d=>(Math.random()*d.Field);
  }
  // select only the items that actually exist
  req = PrivacyProfile.table
    .filter(d=>req.includes(d.Field))
    .map(d=>d.Field)
    ;
  // prepare the return
  let rtn = { req: req };
  // calculate the privacy factor
  rtn.score = rtn.req.reduce((a,d)=>
      a*PrivacyProfile.hashed[d]['PrivacyFactor']
    ,1);
  // if the factor is so small as to require a
  // scientific notation, let's just call it zero
  // This convention is only in place to make reading
  //the results easier
  rtn.score = rtn.score.toString().includes('e') ?
    0 : rtn.score;
  // get the filtered dataset
  rtn.data = basedata.map(d=>{
    d = rtn.req.reduce((a,f)=>a[f] = d[f],{});
    // generate a random id for each record
    d = Object.assign({
        id: Math.floor(
          Math.random()
          *
          Number.MAX_SAFE_INTEGER).toString(32)
      },d);
    return d;
  });
  return rtn;
}
```

This generic function takes a list of variables the analyst wants access to, calculates the cumulative score, and produces the requested dataset. This can then be used to make a request (R00001) for items we know are more generic fields.

```
R00001 = GenerateReqest(['gender','age','hobbies']);
// {
//   req: ["gender", "age", "hobbies"],
//   score: 0.8534004245932628
// }
```

Again, the results match our expectations. We know that gender, age and hobbies have a much higher Privacy Factor and should, therefore, be much safer. However, now that we have a clear measure, we can be more explicit and state that the cumulative product of the request has a Privacy Factor of 0.8534.

Another Data Analyst may make an innocent request for data that surprises us.

```
R00002 =
  GenerateReqest(['state','municipality','registered']);
// {
//   req: ['state','municipality','registered'],
//   score: 0.006712926793301226
// }
```

Their intent is a longitudinal study of the organization's successes and failures. Intuitively, a city should be reasonably anonymous. Surprisingly—likely due to our small data size—this request shows a significantly lower Privacy Factor (0.0067).

394

The Privacy Team should examine this request much more closely to determine if there is a problem and if any further transforms can be applied to the dataset that would reduce the risk profile of the supplied dataset.

Using the Thresholds in Automated Checks

There is no point in having this tool if we can't use it in our systems to make our lives easier. We have already discussed using it to assist in evaluation, but applying it as an automated check is also possible. By setting a predefined threshold, we can perform an automated check on our datasets to ensure that requests are immediately rejected if they are below a predetermined value.

While no single threshold is suitable for all cases, organizations can inspect sample requests to identify an appropriate point for automatic approval, automatic rejection, or calls for further inspection. These thresholds can be applied at different points in the approval chain.

1.   Creating the Request

2.   Privacy Approval

3.   Data generation

When the data analyst begins to put their request together, we can offer them an estimate of the privacy factor of their request. As an inexpensive calculation, this can be done live, during the request process, through a web or application interface. This lets the customer get early feedback about their requests, enabling them to plan their justifications or mitigating transforms that may reduce the risk profile. Assuming the Privacy Threshold is above a predetermined safe threshold, the request can be delivered immediately with no further review.

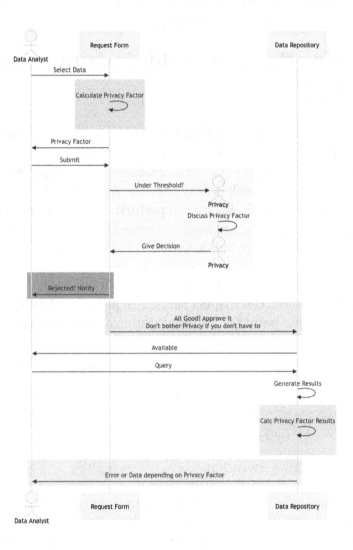

Upon submission of a request requiring further review, Privacy Evaluators can have the privacy estimate available to them as a holistic estimate of the risks involved. This offers a tool to formulate their thoughts; it gives them a metric that allows them to focus on problem areas. This also has the benefit of reducing evaluator bias, where one evaluator may personally have a different risk tolerance than another evaluator. This metric can form the basis for discussion among evaluators and with the customer to focus discussion on real (rather than perceived) issues.

Lastly, we can continue evaluating results even as the customer performs their transforms. It is possible for a dataset to be approved for use, with the understanding that the trusted analyst will perform aggregation that will increase the Privacy Factor of the dataset, but how do we know that they succeeded? If the calculation is performed on a platform we control, we can use these same measures to evaluate the produced dataset. This evaluation can even go further, using a more complete evaluation of the privacy, rather than the estimate we used to get this far.

If their privacy measures are unsuccessful and we control the platform, we can issue an error message indicating that the privacy threshold was unmet.

Judging the appropriate threshold for any given system will be contextual. Privacy analysts will need to evaluate where the cut-off should lie based on the shares' openness and the nature of the data. Secure data managed in secure facilities will require fewer checks than data being published openly on the web.

Conclusion

The ability to measure data anonymity before any requests for access offers several advantages in managing Data Repositories. Claude Shannon's concept of information entropy gives us just such a mechanism, which measures the amount of entropy in a potential channel (shared dataset).

Using this estimate, combined with an evaluation of appropriate thresholds, it is possible to partially automate the approval mechanism for data shares. While complete automation is not possible, we can still reduce the burden on Privacy experts and use these objective measures to reduce the impact of any personal biases the experts may have.

We all recognize the importance of maintaining people's privacy and securing assets in shared datasets. These processes and techniques are useful in helping to reduce costs through objective techniques.

Going a Little Further

While this was an interesting idea to pursue, there are so many more layers that weren't covered.

- **Privacy Weights**: every field should have a manually set weight associated with it. Immediately, this can include values that look unique but will be made available with other protections. For example, a Unique ID should be transformed for every request, so the privacy factor is likely known beforehand but is not represented by the actual data. Having some manually set adjustments can compensate for that.

- **Anonymity Functions**: The initial request could include several very simple and automatically applicable functions. Rounding all dollar figures to the nearest thousandth or including only the first three letters of a name will drastically change the privacy factor.

- **The Thing I Forgot**: I'm sure you could make a million little inclusions to a Data Request that would allow for more refined automation and control. Feel free to drop them in the comments.

Further Reading

Some general articles that appeared in Google searches while I was writing this looked interesting. I read them later.

 A Gentle Introduction to Information Entropy

 On privacy, research, and privacy research. A blog discussing various aspects of data privacy

While we discussed measuring entropy to ensure it was sufficient, there are several things you can do to artificially increase entropy when it is not sufficient.

 Statistical approaches to de-identification, Utrecht University: Discusses various methods for de-identifying data: K-anonymity, L-diversity, T-closeness, and Differential privacy.

I really found Utrecht's book on the matter interesting. As I was looking for references to help make points, I kept referring back to this book.

400

The Evils of Sequential IDs

3 reasons not to use Sequential IDs as Primary Keys

- Sequential IDs have several re-occurring risks that are known

- We will discuss 3 risks associated with Sequential IDs as Primary Keys

- Some valid cases for maintaining Sequential numbers are discussed

2001 was an exciting time for me.

I had just made a significant career change, realizing Nursing was not my thing; I had changed fields and graduated with a CompSci degree, formalizing everything I had tried to teach myself. The Y2K panic had happened, and the DOTCOM bubble had just burst, flooding the field with people with much more experience than I did and making finding a job all the more challenging. 9/11 brought security into crystal focus for professionals everywhere, information security being part of that. In this context, I found my start with a small consulting company that helped small businesses transition from in-house software solutions to robust managed solutions and further into online solutions available anywhere.

During one of these conversions, the owner of my company brought up an article he had recently read, and a debate ensued. According to the article, people should stop using sequential IDs for record identifiers. This seemed absurd to me: Sequence IDs are easy to create and easier to read; it makes no difference what you use internally. He was being absurd.

Unfortunately, he lost the debate.

1. I have long since learned to be more open in my discussions

2. He was right

Many years later, I was working on refactoring a website. I knew there were several vulnerabilities, but time is a precious resource, and I prioritized them as best I could. That's when we got the report; a customer had noticed that when you log in, you get logged into Company 5; he assumed that if there is a 5, there must also be a 6... and he gained access to data he had no business seeing.

If I had been more open to my boss's argument, I might have seen how risky sequential IDs are and prioritized that particular issue more highly.

This issue was not unique to the system I was working on. Almost a decade later, I was in a team-building exercise: an intro C# class. It was all fairly basic stuff, but one thing stuck out... right in the Microsoft-branded textbook: the instructor pointed out a recommendation to use UUIDs for primary keys in your database.

The reason was simple: at some point, a PK will get exposed and act as the starting point for people to derive further information.

The very solution my boss had proposed to a problem I had dismissed. This problem is so widespread that it was necessary to discuss it in introductory programming classes, and the issues with it are obvious to anyone who has grown up in this modern data security and privacy world!

So ... why do we still need to be reminded? Why are we so obsessed with putting numbers in order?

False sense of utility

One argument often raised in favour of sequential IDs is the familiarity of numbers that are in order. This is expressed as

- We have a sense of how many records there are

- It gives me a way to orient myself

- Numbers are easier to read

People are expressing emotional states: we are pattern-seeking monkeys, and seeing ordinal growth gives us a sense of comfort. As hard as it is, the data is not there to satisfy our psychological comfort; instead, we are experts who deal with the uncomfortable realities of data.

This puts us in a tough place. Humans are really good at post hoc rationalizations. Any time we experience discomfort, we will reach for the comfortable and justify it to ourselves in any way we can. Post hoc rationalization is a problem we must each individually struggle with. It's been a while since I've read The Righteous Mind[123], but Haidt always nails this point[124].

> Haidt invokes an evolutionary hypothesis.... Reason, in this view, evolved to help us spin, not to help us learn.[125]

We cannot allow ourselves to use what is comfortable but rather to become comfortable with the most appropriate techniques. To do that, we need to take time to consider the benefits.

---

[123] The Riteous Mind, Jonathan Haidt
https://www.amazon.ca/Righteous-Mind-Divided-Politics-Religion/dp/0307455777
[124] Post Hoc Rationalisation – Reasoning Our Intuition and Changing Our Minds, Jonathan MS Pearce, 2013-11-14
https://skepticink.com/tippling/2013/11/14/post-hoc-rationalisation-reasoning-our-intuition-and-changing-our-minds/
[125] Why Won't They Listen, NYTimes, William Saletan, 2012-03-23
https://www.nytimes.com/2012/03/25/books/review/the-righteous-mind-by-jonathan-haidt.html

If we use a sequence of numbers as a primary key, we use arbitrary keys. Ergo, these are not for human consumption, and therefore, they should not make your reading easier; their purpose is to make the computer's reading easier (and, thus, hopefully, our maintenance).

A critical touch-point in software development, expressed mainly from the perspective of <u>Functional Programming</u>, is to avoid side effects. Each command and function should do one thing and should not be used to affect the system beyond what was specified.

When searching for the above link, Google gave me a sidebar that stated

> Side effects are any changes in the state of the program or the environment that are not reflected in the function's output. Side effects can make the program unpredictable, hard to test, and difficult to debug.

We do not want to become dependent on side effects because, by definition, more than one effect comes from a single action. We cannot change the action to accommodate one effect because that would impact the other.

Using the Primary Key as a sequence? You can't change its data type to something else if necessary because that would make it non-sequential. Need to modify the order? It is not possible; it has foreign key references.

Our job, as experts, is not to define data in ways that make us comfortable; rather, it is our job to define data as it is.

> define whatever it is we perceive — to trace its
> outline — so we can see what it really is: its
> substance. Stripped bare. As a whole. Unmodified.
> And to call it by its name — the thing itself and its
> components ... Nothing is so conducive to spiritual
> growth as this capacity for logical and accurate
> analysis of everything that happens to us.
>
> — Meditations 3.11[126]

Risks

Security

The two main examples from my personal experience
draw on the security risk associated with sequential
numbers. Sequences of numbers give us a pattern that we
can use to predict the next or previous value.

Whether we meant to or not, by using sequential IDs, we
have introduced information into our dataset.

In exposed applications that control information, this has
been known to hint to people that more information is
available.

In Nova Scotia in 2018, an individual using a government
data transfer system[127] noticed that the numbers were
relatively small when retrieving FOIP information releases

---

[126] Meditations, Emperor of Rome Marcus Aurelius
https://gutenberg.org/ebooks/2680

[127] Concerns teen being 'railroaded' in privacy breach to
cover government slip, Jon Tattrie, CBC News, 2018-04-12
https://www.cbc.ca/news/canada/nova-scotia/concerns-t
een-being-railroaded-in-privacy-breach-to-cover-gove
rnment-slip-1.4616972

online. He surmised that the numbers were sequential and tried to type the following number into his browser. He was surprised when he got a FOIP record that did not belong to him. His guess would likely have resulted in a miss if non-sequential values had been used. The large spaces with non-valid values would have been missed.

Clicking on the item's link brings the user to the item's page and puts the URL for that item, including its unique identification number, in the browser's address bar. Changing just the number in the address bar takes the user to a different item directly

— OIPC Investigation Report[128]

While this type of risk is well known, it remains common, but at least it is obvious. Unfortunately, there are far more insidious ways in which data leaks occur.

Sequential IDs can be exploited statistically to gain estimates of total counts. This is known as The German Tank Problem.

During WWII, it was necessary to identify how many tanks Germany produced. Using the serial numbers off the wheels of destroyed tanks, analysts could estimate the total number of wheels (and, therefore, tanks) in operation.

---

[128] Office of the Information and Privacy Commissioner for Nova Scotia INVESTIGATION REPORT IR19-01 Department of Internal Services Freedom of Information Access (FOIA) Website Catherine Tully Information and Privacy Commissioner for Nova Scotia https://oipc.novascotia.ca/sites/default/files/publications/OIPC%20Investigation%20Report%20IR19-01%20%2815%20Jan%202019%29.pdf

> wheels, which were observed to be sequentially numbered ... Analysis of wheels from two tanks ... yielded an estimate of 270 tanks produced in February 1944 ... German records after the war showed production for the month of February 1944 was 276
>
> — <u>German Tank Problem</u>, Wikipedia

Randomly selecting a sample and then looking at their sequence numbers gives us an idea of how dense the population is. We can estimate population (and sub-population) size from a sample using one of <u>several functions</u>.

When we share large datasets for analysis, we often exclude records deemed to be outside the Data Scientist's domain of interest (often for privacy). Unfortunately, if we share underlying sequential values, we expose more information about the more extensive set than we intended. The customer can derive information about the unshared portion of the data.

Distributed Systems

In the early 90s, the <u>Open Source Foundation (OSF)</u> released the <u>Distributed Computing Environment</u>, bringing large-scale computing systems to the fore. Suddenly, individual analysts were not tied to their local desktops and could distribute their processing across unlimited computers and processors. While less readily available than modern Cloud services, intra-organizational processing became much more powerful.

One problem that arose from using distributed compute systems is that it takes time for the processing units to talk to each other. To optimize a distributed solution, the processing units must be able to act independently of each other as much as possible.

Unfortunately, sequential keys require coordination. At the very least, a single computer must touch every record to coordinate the generation of the next value.

This acts as a bottleneck in processing.

For the processing units to assign a coordinated value, they must communicate with each other to serialize the values. This means that either the sequential value must be added to the records before distributing the data (requiring the cost of producing a new dataset), or the values must be assigned in blocks (effectively randomly across partitions)

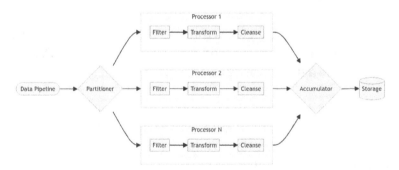

The goal is to get data onto the distributed processors with as little fuss as possible.

While the OSF came up with an exciting solution to this problem, random numbers and cryptographic hashes have become more prevalent in the intervening decades. Using huge random numbers, we can be reasonably assured that the number generated will be unique to the population, meaning there is no need to coordinate between systems. Each processor can independently assign identifiers without concerning itself with the work of other processors in the system. The results can later be merged as one step.

Hashes serve a similar purpose but have the benefit of being deterministic. It is possible to process a unit and identify which unit it is without having to do expensive scanning on the more extensive set. Suppose some data feature can be used as a unique identifier; hashes can be utilized to convert that feature into a reasonably sized and well-distributed integer suitable for use as a key[129]. Like random numbers, we can be assured that there will not be a conflicting number. Still, we also have the benefit of being able to integrate overlapping entities if they are determined to represent the same thing.

Imbalanced Indexes

The Law of Threes dictates that I make three subpoints, so I had to devise a third reason not to use Sequential IDs. This one is a little more of a stretch.

There is an argument that sequential IDs do not balance well in the binary tree during partitioning for storage, processing, or indexing of datasets. This first came up during a (now lost) lecture I watched by Damien Katz (I think) of IBM regarding CouchDB. He discussed why random keys were important to database performance and asked audience members if their keys became imbalanced. This highlighted issues I remember from Project Gutenberg's data store in which they partition based on

---

[129] See chapter "De-duplicating Data Storage in Data Science"

the first digit of the sequential number of the book submission.

Under these conditions, <u>Benford's Law</u> is going to burn us.

Benford's Law states that a number's first digit is often low. In a sequential set, it is obvious why this would be true: every time you change scales (say 1's to 10's), it takes ten times longer to change the first digit (in other cases, this remains a mystery to me).

For partitioning, the first partition will get 30% of the work, while partition 9 will only receive 5%, creating massive bottlenecks while one grinds away and another sits idle.

While I have seen real-world examples of this and do recognize the problem as a problem, I am generally dismissive of it. Implementing a fast, balanced hashing algorithm that resolves this problem is relatively simple.

Using the example from above, Benford's Law can be circumvented by simply reversing the numbers (effectively a `Mod10` hash). So instead of sending the sequence `[101, 102, 103, 104, 105]` to the same partition, we are better off using `[101, 201, 301, 401, 501]` to distribute the values more evenly.

Having come across articles on the hashing algorithms used in indexing by some of the big database engines, I expect data balancing during partitioning to be a well-understood and handled problem in any platform I adopt. If you have to balance your values, these may be valid considerations, but looking at your chosen tools may be in order.

Valid Uses

As with any absolute rule ... well ... there is no such thing as an absolute rule. There are exceptions and valid reasons for why you might want a sequential identifier.

Audits

Going back to my very early days in my career, when my colleagues and I were just trying to figure out how to turn a dollar, a few of us took to teaching How to use Office night classes at local community centres, job retraining centres, or (mine) crime exit programs; all of us had a module Use Excel to Make an Invoice.

One weekend, I was at one of these friends' houses. We were having a few beers and working on a hobby problem together when he mentioned a lesson he had learned from one of his students.

As part of his invoice class, he taught how to make invoice numbers automatically (`last inv number + 1`), but he told the class, "If you want to make your business look more impressive to your customers, change that formula to `last inv number + 10`. Even if you only have one customer, it won't look that way."

A hand near the back slowly went up.

"I am an accountant and have to recommend people not to do that. When you undergo a tax audit, they will identify the gaps as *missing invoices* and assume you have done 10x as much business as you have reported. They will estimate what those invoices are worth and send you a bill for the apparently missing nine invoices."

That's something you want to avoid, but the ability to match patterns and find gaps, which poses the original risk, also has benefits. The main reason I will reach for a sequential ID is for audit purposes: a sequential ID can verify missing data by creating gaps in the sequence when data is removed.

You want to avoid that, but the ability to match patterns and find gaps, which poses the original risk, also has benefits. The main reason I will reach for a sequential ID is for audit purposes: a sequential ID can verify missing data by creating gaps in the sequence when data is removed.

Non-technical individuals often don't understand how malleable information[130] is in a digital world[131]; it is easier for them to comprehend that the number has incremented than it is to understand a chain of hashes (Merkle Trees), so adding a sequence ID for visiting auditors can be a courtesy.

Replication Checkpoints

One of the databases I like to use a lot is CouchDB, and one of its super-powers is its ability to replicate the data across multiple peers.

---

[130] The Wayback Machine of The Internet Archive demonstrates the maleability of web content. It is an independant archive showing when websites have changed their content. Often this is the only record that a change has been made.
https://web.archive.org/
[131] See Chapter "Paper as a Digital Storage Medium" for ways to manage malleable digital information

To achieve this, a few things must occur to address conflict resolution, change histories, and split brains[132], but one of the critical elements is the simplest: every change to the database gets a sequence number[133].

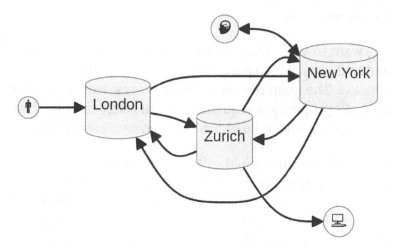

This number is used during replication to act as a bookmark, allowing one database to request every change since a point in time.

This is an essential tool to be used during replication, being able to state: give me everything since checkpoint X.

A similar construct is also available in MS SQL Server, called a `rowversion` (it was a `timestamp` last I used it). I'm sure most other DBs have the same concept: a globally incrementing sequence.

---

[132] The split-brain problem is one in which two copies of a database are receiving updates but not able to communicate with one another.
https://guide.couchdb.org/editions/1/en/conflicts.html
[133] Replication, CouchDB Manual
https://guide.couchdb.org/editions/1/en/replication.html#magic

Solutions

Given all of this, what should we do when constructing identifiers?

Big Integers

No matter what identifier style you use, make sure you use big integers.

In those early days of web applications, our databases had auto-incrementing indexes that could have been randomly specified as the sequence. However, they were constrained to a 32-bit integer, with only room for about 4 billion records.

Not a lot by modern standards.

If you use random numbers, you only benefit from the gaps if they are reasonably large. If you use sequential values, you do not want to run out.

Random values, Hashes, and UUIDs

Generally, I suggest using (at least) a 128-bit integer for storage. I don't choose this number arbitrarily; yes, it's large, but it is also the size of a UUID. This has the convenience of having a ready-to-use storage type on most systems and standardized functions for generating random (or near-random) numbers of that size.

I say near random because while UUIDv4 is a random number, other versions of UUID are not. For example, version 1 depended on the computer's MAC address to form part of its uniqueness. Further, some implementations of UUID generators are not truly standards conformant; instead, they include timestamps in the number for convenience.

Hashes are another interesting option; while deterministic, they are effectively random. If a dataset has a natural key that we do not necessarily want to share but makes an obvious primary key, hashes can be a convenient way to mask the natural key. It generates a large (effectively) random integer. While an `md5` will fit into a 128-bit integer, most modern hashes require more space.

 One exciting benefit of using a hash occurs when you require scrambling of your keys. Using a <u>salt value</u> (perhaps a salt value per customer), we can allow for simple regeneration of different random-like keys if we ever require them to change.

Primary Keys must never be sequential

There are reasons to use sequential numbers, but making a primary lookup value creates the temptation to expose it to the client, and the moment you have something that looks tempting, it will happen. Let me say that again:

Your primary key will be exposed to the customer.

There are all kinds of reasons we promise it won't, but at some point, somebody will make a mistake and expose that number. After all, it is the value we look at in individual records. If for no other reason than an analyst wants to do a join against two tables, that primary key is going to get exposed.

By using random-like values for PKs, there is less *temptation* to utilize them for inappropriate things. We can only derive information from them indirectly and,

416

therefore, don't try to use them for secondary purposes. If we need to add sequential values, put them in a field that explicitly defines why they exist, clarifying their purpose (and non-purpose).

Non-primary, Unique Identifiers

Just keep an eye out for them.

Do you have a field called `created_time`?

If your data has a creation timestamp, it may have something very close to a unique identifier. While this may not be sensitive information, users can use it to join data against other datasets.

While useful for diagnostic purposes, these low entropy values pose a risk when exposed to the broader customer group. We can simply remove these values from data shares by not having them as the primary key. By having these unique values not acting as primary keys, we are not bound by their side effects and are less tempted to share them inappropriately.

If these values are required for diagnostics, then we must maintain them. Our only defence is to be aware of the risks and keep the values unbound and hidden from the shared datasets.

Conclusion

While there are valid reasons for maintaining sequential values in data, using sequential values as the primary key poses significant risks to data. Given the nature of primary identifiers, the cost of the risks versus the perceived benefits does not justify their use.

Separating valid sequential use cases from the primary identifier allows us to separate the concerns of the data's purpose, allowing us to move parts independently of side effects. Large integers have been widely available for over 30 years, allowing us to create significant gaps of negative space in our data to evade malicious detection. Modern random number generation and cryptographic hashes offer a secure way to populate that large space.

Given these simple and well-established solutions, the risks to security and performance posed by using sequential primary keys do not outweigh their perceived benefits.

As engineers and architects, we need to consider not how we have always perceived data but rather the historical and scientific context surrounding protecting that data. The security mechanisms of the past no longer suit the computational realities of the present.

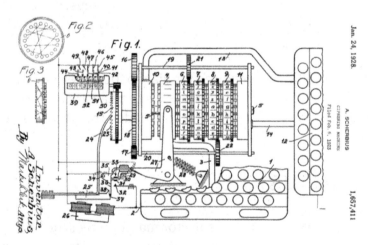

1928 US patent 1,657,411: Enigma Cypher Machine

Conclusion

You're still here?

Wow, that's really cool.

One of the obstacles to change in the office is being willing to work to understand the system around us. People quickly hang their brains on a coat hook at the door to get through the day without struggling and hoping to avoid conflict. If you've made it this far, you have demonstrated something more than that.

Persistence, or what some might call 'Bloody-Mindedness', is the key to unlocking the mysteries of the complex system around us. It's this unwavering determination that will enable you to comprehend the generic components of these systems, and ultimately, to effect change.

When I embarked on this journey, I must admit, I didn't anticipate much. But I've always harboured a deep passion for change and a fervent desire to see the world transform for the better. Your presence here, your commitment to understanding and changing complex systems, has truly surprised and inspired me. You've shown that you're the kind of person who can make a tangible difference in this world. And that, my friends, fills me with joy.

Whether you are a manager trying to gain insight into your team's challenges or a student looking at the issues you will face, Information Systems are no longer external to our lives and careers but are the business processes themselves. I hope you gained a general perspective of the world of information systems and how they integrate (or don't integrate) directly into our lives.

If these chapters prepared you for the exciting challenges and opportunities around you ... well ... mission accomplished.

-A-
Astrolabe: Tips For Teachers

1. As an introduction, promise students that in the next 30 minutes they are going build their first computer program.

2. Don't have students cut-out the circles. By keeping them on the page, you imply no rotation. This delays discovery long enough for you to suggest it as intentional thought.

3. Students will have different tightness of their spirals. This is a hint as to the trade-off between high differentiation, and more colours.

4. There will be the student that is tentative about punching a hole in their paper. The hole needs to be big enough that the colour shows through. Encouraging the student to be a little rough with it gets a couple of chuckles.

5. Have the students (as a group) describe how their computer meets the three criteria that were laid out.

6. Ignore the aesthetics until the very end. Inevitably a student will bring up aesthetics. Act surprised... like you forgot about it. Then hold up your demo and rotate it. If you don't like the palette you got, turn it to select a different palette.

7. Like any activity, leave this to the end of the class. The excitement caused by comparing colour schemes brings the class to an end. Expect to do no more than have students take a written handout on the way out the door.

8. At the beginning, you drew a spiral. This was not strictly necessary. Really, you should do this using Radial Coordinate graphs (on paper), or a continuous formula. The act of counting across, and in, was the real spiral algorithm.

Activity Plan

Skills

- Algorithmic Thinking

- Problem definition

Learning Objectives

- Describe the use of colour in categorisation

- Describe the components of a good colour palette

- Apply the components of a good colour palette

Audience

- Grades 7 — Undergraduate
- Introductory programming students
- Introductory data analysis students

Materials

- Colour Wheel: Make one, or print the templates
- Radial graph: must be same size as colour wheel
- Pencil: must be sharp

Progression

1. Learn the three components of a good colour palette (~5 min)
2. Construct a colour selector (~5 min)
3. Reflect

Steps

1. Gather Supplies (pencil/printouts)
2. All the way across, 1 over, step in, Repeat until full
3. Punch Holes
4. Select colours, record by colouring in grid

Reflection/Assessment

- What changes could you make to get even more colours?

- What happens to differentiation as you get more colours?

- What decision making inputs can you control on the machine?

- How can you change the colours if they aren't aesthetically pleasing?

www.ingramcontent.com/pod-product-compliance
Lightning Source LLC
Chambersburg PA
CBHW070931050326
40689CB00014B/3159